DISCOVER FULFILLED LIVING

by

EVELYN CORRADO

ISBN-978-1-910256-46-6

Praise for 'Discover Fulfilled Living'…..

I have been privileged to be approached by Evelyn Corrado to have a first look at her book, Discover Fulfilled Living, before publishing. It is an honour for which I am truly thankful.

Discover Fulfilled Living is insightful, well written and researched, and it could give different people inspiration to face their lives with renewed hope. The topic of all-round well-being and self-esteem is one that has been tackled by many writers, all trying to make sense of the great conundrum that is the human condition. No one solution is, however, universally final, as every single person is different in their situation, their attitudes and values. It is therefore one topic that needs revisiting and re-adjusting through the ages, as humans evolve and change with the changing world.

I therefore think Evelyn's words of advice will find a mark in some people's lives and hopefully give them ideas for the new approach that they need to overcome their individual bug-bears and change their lives. Her book is relevant and on point, dealing with the pressures and problems of modern life.

Discover fulfilled Living is an inspiring and well-thought out effort by Evelyn, and I would recommend it to anyone who wants to improve their life simply by changing the way they view themselves and the world they live in.

Njoki Kamau, Author

AUTHOR'S SPECIAL THANK YOU NOTE.

I would like to specially express gratitude to my family for their great support, particularly my mum Justina, who has always encouraged me to endeavour and achieve. I also acknowledge the great support of my wonderful husband Luca, who whole heartedly supported this project. Thank you to my mentors, Author Njoki Kamau and Dr Michael Kihara for insight.

After many years of psychology studies and working in mental health, I compile this book that holistically addresses important areas of life, in order to help individuals' achieve Fulfilled Living. Overall, it doesn't matter where you come from, or your circumstances. If you apply the right principles of life, you can constructively change your world and of those around you.

I specially **dedicate** this book to my nephew Titus, who is part of our future generation.

CONTENTS

INTRODUCTION

One summer afternoon as I came off a train from London underground, I noticed a lady struggling to carry her baby's buggy up the stairs, as a crying child trailed behind her desperately. As a good Samaritan, I asked the lady if I could assist her carry the buggy up the stairs. To my amazement she declined my offer, but repeatedly thanked me.

I decided to continue with my journey and mind my own business, but I could not avoid wondering why she declined my help. She was obviously struggling and appreciated support, that's why she was grateful for my offer, but she was too proud or possibly too shy to accept it or could be she didn't trust me.

Many of us like the lady might be in the same boat needing help or changes in our lives, but we are too proud to admit it to others or even to ourselves. Nonetheless, when we bottle up issues, they have a way of coming out and exposing us to the very people we were hiding them from.

Looking around our world today, there are many people looking like they have it all together, but they are silently struggling in their relationships, finances and also living stressful, unhappy lifestyles. Eventually, when it is too late they are faced by life crises like relationships breakdown, divorce, debt crisis, depression and other health problems either mental or physical.

Are you trying too much to keep it together, yet you feel frustrated, tired and never doing enough?

This book is for you. It helps you realise areas in your life that need attending to, to maintain balance. Additionally, it will aid you to identify the clutter you need to cut out from your life. This will lead you to enjoy living a healthy, happier and successful life.

We all go to school and spend a lot of years learning skills for our careers, jobs and business. But we spend less time or no time learning life skills or health knowledge on how to maintain our self-esteem in crisis, or on how to overcome trauma and abuse. Generally, we rarely learn how to manage our resources which include time, finances, character, talent and relationships. Then, later in life despite having progressed in age and career, we still find it difficult to get along with others. In some cases we earn a lot of money but we end up in financial crisis.

Sometimes, we are very good at our jobs but we can't keep our marriages and family contented. Other times despite good academic and career success, we get so stressed that we end up depressed, losing the pleasure of all we worked for throughout our life.

Failure in life comes from **deception, ignorance and distraction.** When we are too busy we lose focus from the important things in life and run around aimlessly. At the end of the day, you find you have achieved nothing of value and you are tired and frustrated. Some of us spend decades running around but in the end we achieve below our potential because we were distracted by the busyness of life. Other times, we are unaware of what is needed to be done in different areas of our lives, so we are ignorant and are easily deceived, for example in areas of health, relationships and life management. Nevertheless, if we seek the correct information and are willing to work hard and make effective changes in our lives, then we can succeed and live happier and healthier lives.

This book gives you practical skills of life that have not been taught in normal academic classes. Most times, these topics are also not addressed in churches or other social and informal gatherings. However they are indispensable for a fulfilled living. The book chapters address key areas of life and give you tips on how to succeed, maintaining life balance, health and happiness. The information is vital for all individuals of all ages.

It addresses key issues relating to;

1. Achieving and maintain healthy living - psychological, emotional and physical health.
2. Building good self-esteem, ego strength, character and independence.

3. Recognizing self-identity – talents, ability, gifts, skills, opportunities and passion.
4. Developing healthy relationships and supportive social structures.
5. Upholding success through strategic goal planning and discipline.
6. Overcoming life setbacks, failure and negative behaviour.
7. Stress management and holistic life balance approach.
8. Keeping up hope, faith and happiness.

From a personal position, I have occasionally been deficient in particular areas addressed in this book, whereas I was good at some areas. Though I am not yet perfect, over time I am more knowledgeable after lots of reading, daily practice and honest self-analysis. Additionally, through observation of others, I have been able to appraise how one can maximise potential whilst identifying mistakes that can be evaded. Hence, as an author I have used personal experiences and knowledge and also those of others as case pointers to help you have a practical outlook.

I am a strong believer in the saying that **'Where there is a will there is a way'**, in fact it is the slogan for my EV-ONLINE COUNSELLING SERVICES. I know when you identify areas that need change and are willing to do what it takes to make amendments, then you shall attain your life goals and maximise potential. Before you proceed into the main chapters of the book, I will give you a simple WELL BEING CHECKLIST that will help you to holistically assess your life and identify areas that need change.

It is imperative for you to distinguish the areas you need to fully focus on. Remember as Mae West stated that *'You only live once, but if you do it right, once is enough.'*

WELL BEING CHECKLIST

MENTAL HEALTH   **YES   NO**

Do you think positive most times

Do you have self-acceptance

Do you enjoy creativity

Are you assertive

Do you enjoy certainty

Is your self-esteem & identity healthy

Do you have good concentration

Is your memory good enough

PHYSICAL HEALTH   **YES   NO**

Do you eat a balance diet

Do you sleep well

Do you exercise regularly

Have you stopped smoking

Do you drink alcohol

Do you have any drug problems

Do you have a good hygiene

Do you have any physical illnesses

GOALS AND SUCCESS   **YES   NO**

Do you have a job

Have you met your life ambitions

Are you learning new skills

Are you studying

Do you feel you work effectively

Do you manage money well

Do you have debts

Do you enjoy your work place

RELATIONS, HOPE AND FAITH   **YES   NO**

Do you have good relationships

Are you close to your family

Do you have friends

Do you have a belief or faith

Do you have trust and hope in life

Are you sociable in a group

Do you have good communication skills

     For one to have a successful, happy and healthy life, one needs to take care of psychological and physical health. At the same time, maintain healthy relationships, have SMART life goals that are well aligned to opportunities and potential ability of the individual. Then above all, be able to have hope and spiritual strength to keeping going in life. Lastly, be able to balance all the areas of life using good stress management skills and finally reach out to help others succeed, as you enjoy a healthy and successful happy life.

CHAPTER 1 : PSYCHOLOGICAL WELLBEING

ABOUT MENTAL HEALTH

As a young person growing up, I discerned a lot of issues of life that left me gobsmacked. I felt the need to understand the causes and cure of some of these problems. Truthfully, it always shocked me to see deprived mothers hardly surviving on the streets of Nairobi, going ahead to give birth to many children, who became street children as we called them in the 1990's.

I questioned why these mothers could be that careless? Why couldn't they use contraceptives or abstain from sex? I wondered.

Additionally, I was astounded by politicians' fantastic pleas to the public during election campaigns, only for them to under deliver once they joined parliament. Nevertheless, the public voted them back again to parliament over and over.

Don't the public learn? Why did they make those choices? I wondered quietly.

I also deliberated within my mind why some couples got married, only to separate unceremoniously a few years later. Likewise, I was marvelled when my college mate committed suicide after breaking up with her boyfriend. How could she do that? Didn't she see how beautiful she was and the bright future she could have had? Why didn't she speak to her friends or to her parents, or to the pastor, or to the college counsellor for support?

More so, I doubted how I could overcome the pain of my dad's death and wondered if life for me could ever become normal again.

These questions among others on the issues of brain, behaviour and life pushed me to study psychology. I hoped that maybe my understanding on psychological wellbeing would be beneficial to me and also to others like you.

Subsequently, having worked in mental health in United Kingdom for a decade, I have recognised that beyond the stigma laid on Mental Health subject, it is paramount for each of us to learn more on how to maintain good psychological wellbeing. Consequently, we all need to overcome stressful and frustrating lifestyles in order to achieve healthier and happier livelihoods. Indeed, the line between good mental health and developing mental health problems is very thin. Hence, we need to address issues of brain and behaviour, so as not to cross the line onto the illness side.

Having a good mental health is being able to think clearly, having good self-esteem, social confidence and not having a mental illness.

Nevertheless, if you have suffered mental health problems it's never too late to adjust, learn and manage the illness better for your future life. We need to know that sometimes we cannot prevent tragedy, but we can prevent the tough times from destroying our lives.

Any human being is prone to mental health problems and depression despite their age, class, race, gender or religion. Nonetheless, most people hide mental health problems for the fear of social stigma. Moreover, if one is not personally affected, there are people close to us who might suffer from the illness and we need to be able to understand and support them, instead of alienating them.

Statistics show that 1 in 4 people will experience a mental health problem in any given year, which is 25% of the population (MIND UK). Women are known to be twice more sufferers than men. Additionally, young adults especially students have been reported to have high rate of depression of 21% in 2011 (NCHA). Hence, mental illness is around us and we can no longer pretend it doesn't exist or that it is far away from us.

Indeed, mental health subject is indispensable because its' knowledge will help us make good decisions in life, which affect every part of our being which includes relationships, career, finances, recreation and achieving healthy lifestyle choices among others. Undeniably, if we do not take care of our brain, mind, behaviour, attitudes and emotions, the repercussions can be critical. I am obligated to start my book with this chapter as it wheels all other parts of our lives. Even though, most of us give the subject less or no attention.

We need to know more about achieving good mental health and also about dealing with issues of emotional and psychological well-being.

Causes of Mental Health issues

a. Environment and Upbringing

When one is exposed for some time to a toxic environment like unhealthy relationship, it can cause mental health problems. An example is one's upbringing can lead to mental health issues if a child was abused or grew up in a dysfunctional environment. Psychologists have outlined how childhood relationships influence individual behaviour throughout life.

Most children who were brought up by a parent with mental health problems or life problems exhibited disorganised and insecure attachments to their children. Hence the children grew up insecure. Most of these children end up with low self-esteem, angry and confused. Some of them end up abusing drugs or having mental health issues like anorexia, self-harm and depression.

Study statistics from Illinois (Sachs& Miller 2011) and also from Kramer and Ellen (2003) have shown that about 62% of women brought up in dysfunctional family ended up either in prostitution or in abusive adult relationships.

Most of us as we grow older we are surprised by how much we become just like our parents. Some of the behaviours we exhibit are the ones we disliked most in our parents, but we unconsciously learned them. According to psychologist Bandura (1977), in his social learning theory, children learn behaviours, emotions and attitudes from observing their care givers, which are later displayed in their own life. Hence, if the parents are dysfunctional, aggressive and violent these behaviours are adopted by their children.

It is therefore important to be aware of our own behaviour and deal with any dysfunctions and try not to transfer the behaviour to our children or to project the behaviour to our friends, colleagues or spouses.

Other environmental factors that can cause mental health are toxic work environments, toxic neighbourhoods and being in abusive relationships. We will cover more on unhealthy relationships and work stressors later in the book, but it is important to note these factors can lead to high stress levels and anxiety. Furthermore, if these issues are not addressed, the anxiety can heighten to mental health problems and even to illnesses like anxiety disorders, depression and psychotic illnesses.

Substance misuse can also lead to mental health problems. Use of illegal drug has caused psychotic episodes to individual for example hearing voices. Some people when they get over the episode they can go back to normal, but if the use of the substances continues the individual can have an irreversible mental health issues. Indeed, especially for people with genetically predisposition of mental illness. Nonetheless, they can live a healthy life if they are stress free and do not use illegal drugs. But use of substances can trigger the mental illnesses.

b. Genetic Pre-disposition

Some mental health problems are genetically predisposed from parental genes. Hence, some individual with illness like Bi-polar depression and schizophrenia could have inherited from their parents. Hence, it is important to be aware of your family history to see if there is a likelihood of carrying mental disorder genes. Nevertheless, it could be minimal and if not triggered by other factors the probability of having a mental illness might be slim. However, it is important to be aware if you or your spouse is carrier of any mental illness, as we do also with the physical health prognosis.

c. Chemical imbalance

Another biological origin of mental health is due to chemical imbalances in the brain. The imbalance of neural-transmitters in the brain (Serotonin and dopamine) can lead to psychiatry problems which cause illness like ADHD (Attention-Deficit Hyperactivity Disorder), depression, paranoia and anxiety. Neural-transmitters' work in the brain is to send signals from one cell nerve to the other. The two major neural transmitters related to brain and mental health are serotonin and dopamine.

i)-Dopamine helps with emotions arousal balance, regulating motor behaviour and motivation. If one has an imbalanced level of dopamine in the brain it can lead to poor focus and illnesses like Parkinson disease ADHD, Schizophrenia among others. The good news is that the levels of dopamine can be readjusted using medication prescribed by psychiatrists.

ii)-Serotonin helps regulate the brain for example sleep, body temperature, libido among other. Hence if it is not balanced, it can lead to illness like OCD (obsessive-compulsive disorder), depression, bulimia, anorexia, insomnia among others.

Prolonged stressful lifestyles can lead to low production of serotonin which can then cause mental health problems and sometime also physical health issues. Use of illegal drugs can also affect the level of neural transmission which can also lead to mental health issues i.e. schizophrenia, depression among others.

d. **Trauma**

Mental health issues can typically start when one is faced with immense life setbacks, for example when going through a traumatic life experience like divorce, financial crisis or diagnosed with a life threatening illness. The physical body and the brain suffer immense stress that can lead to mental break down. Other traumatic episodes that can lead to mental health issues are like car accident, being in a war environment, brain damage from a fall, rape, sexual assault or getting shocking news like death of a loved one or a relationship break up or loss of property. These incidents can lead to PSTD (Post Traumatic Stress Disorder) which requires therapy. As noted earlier, stress management issues will be addressed later in the book.

Overall, some of the mental illnesses we know are depression, personality disorders, anxiety disorders, PSTD, eating disorders and psychotic illness like schizophrenia. Most of these illnesses are genetically predisposed to individuals and other causes are due to the factors outlined above. These diagnoses can be medically addressed through psychotic medications, also through psychological therapy and also through adopting healthier life styles.

When one is diagnosed with an illness, the doctor is obligated to give them all the information related to the disease and they should provide support. I will not outline into details different diagnosis of mental illness, but if you think you have any issues I advise you to see your doctor for assistance.

I will discuss different issues of brain and behaviour which can lead to mental health issues. Sometimes we neglect the small foxes and they end up spoiling the whole vine.

As the author of Leadership skills John Maxwell stated 'The greatest day in your life and mine, is the day when we take total responsibility for our attitudes and behaviour. That is the day we truly grow up'. Hence, these areas addressed in the book are very important for all those who want to take responsibility of their mental health. These areas can affect normal people functioning well in the society, however they can limit them from fully enjoying their lives. Additionally, they can lead them to getting into problems like addictions, debt, relationship crises and eventually they can end up with mental illnesses.

Major areas of Psychological wellbeing-:

i) Self-Esteem

ii) Anger

iii) Depression

i) BUILDING A GOOD SELF-ESTEEM

Before moving abroad I fitted quite well in my Kenyan community, but once I stepped onto the European soil I felt different. My skin colour and accent were different from most people around me and in some cases the distinction was incriminating. Although most people were friendly and accommodating, some people looked quite uncomfortable with my presence.

I encountered strange questions, for example some asked me if I had used a fridge before, or if it ever rained in Kenya, or whether my skin colour came off when I took showers. I did not blame the people who questioned me, since I understood their curiosity and also their source of biased information from the media about Africa. Still, occasionally I was left gobsmacked with feelings of insecurity and anger.

One peculiar encounter happened at the city of Dundee, when a stranger approached me and asked if I felt hotter than the rest of the crowd since I was dark skinned. I found his behaviour very offensive but I decided to remain silent to avoid an altercation in public.

Over the years at different places, I have been treated differently. At times, I have been called unpleasant names for being a different colour skin. Nevertheless, I have made a conscious decision to not let anyone determine my value, or to deter my esteem. I have succeeded in controlling my feelings and in choosing the appropriate responses. I have worked hard to maintain good esteem by appropriately addressing unhealthy emotions that might have negative effect on me. This is because I understood that *"One's dignity may be assaulted, vandalized and cruelly mocked, but it can never be taken away, unless it is surrendered."* M.Fox.

I will share tips I have learnt from my own experiences and also from my observations of others while I worked in therapy. I have met a lot of people whose emotional and psychological health is deterred, but they are not willing to change due to fear, lack of information and also procrastination. However change is inevitable, as Marilyn Fergusson stated *'Ultimately we know deeply that the other side of every fear is freedom'*.

Self-esteem is an evaluation of self, which affects how we feel most of the times and also how we interact with others. Everyone has a need to feel valued by self and others. However, it's one's responsibility to maintain good self-esteem. A healthy self-esteem can be cultivated through positive behaviour and engagements that raises one's feelings of self-value and confidence.

Low self-esteem can originate from bad experiences, sometimes in childhood or in any other stage of life. A good example is where a child grows up with an abusive parent who constantly tells them they are not good enough. The child is told he/she is a failure and would not amount to anything. These experiences make one feel worthless or unwanted and not valued. Subsequently, the experience creates an unconscious negative core-belief, which is projected in the feelings and behaviours of the individual throughout their life if the issue is not addressed.

Most negative encounters lead to negative core-beliefs which make one to feel low. As a result, the person tries to cover up by trying too much to please the person or to prove to themselves otherwise. Indeed, some children have tried to work so hard to please the disapproving parent or teacher or role model. The individual ultimately can become workaholic or a perfectionist or obsessed with particular behaviour. Furthermore, if the person encounters another bad experience in life that proves they were not good enough, they end up adopting destructive behaviour like aggression, self-harm, alcoholism or substance abuse. In summary, the individual is suffering from low esteem as a result of a bad experience, which leads to the individual adopting negative core beliefs that lead to destructive behaviour and the cycle repeats itself.

Likewise, interacting with people who constantly put you down can generate a low self-esteem. For example at school when one is bullied at work or even in other social situations or when one is being intimidated by others. The feelings of insecurity rises up if the occurrence is constant then the victim can adopt low self-esteem.

Some personalities are more prone to low self-esteem than others especially among introverts who find it difficult to engage in social gathering or in phlegmatic who dislike disagreeing with other people. Personalities that are outgoing might also suffer low self-esteem if they feel rejected or misunderstood by others. They might try to cover up their feelings by over engaging or by drinking to be more sociable. Other times they can try to be more pleasing.

One needs to be aware of environments that enhance feelings of low self-worth, for example toxic work place or abusive relationships. Still, bad encounters and life setbacks can affect one's self-esteem negatively, for example if one fail an exam they might find it difficult to feel confident with their capability. Also if a mother miscarry a child, she might feel depressed and have a low self-esteem.

During these challenging times one always needs support to get through the situation and also to cultivate back healthy esteem. It is the responsibility of the people around the individual to be supportive.

Other causes of low self-esteem;

As noted earlier being subject to **abuse** – sexual, emotional or physical, and the loss of control leads to low self-esteem. If one is abused as a child or at any point in their life, the traumatic experience leaves the victim's self-image distorted and most times destroyed. Some people identify with the experience as a result and can have a lot of emotional problems.

Having your physical and emotional **needs neglected in childhood** by those close to you especially parents can be detrimental to your self-esteem. Parents who exhibit dysfunctional attachments and care towards their children lead to these children to have low self-esteem.

Failing to meet the **expectations of your parents** who are authoritarian and demanding. Authoritarian parent push their children to follow their dream even when the child find it extremely stressed. Some of these parents are suffering from low self-esteem from past failure or previous negative experiences of poverty or authoritarian background. Hence, they push their children to reach their dreams or to keep up with their own success.

Nonetheless, the children constantly feel inadequate and in a dilemma on how to satisfy their parent who seems not easily pleased. Hence, the children grow up with low esteem since they feel like they are not good enough. Some can be subjected in dreams they are not mentally or physically capable to accomplish. Some of these children if care is not taken they can develop not only low esteem but also have other health issues like gastric ulcers, eating disorders, anxiety issues, depression and in extreme cases can become suicidal.

Feeling like the 'odd one out' at school- most people who have been bullied or felt they were different at school and could not fit in have suffered low esteem. A good example is when one was taller or bigger in size than the other kids, if one has a disability or has suffered emotional issues. Another example is my earlier illustration of how I initially felt alienated in a foreign land (Europe). The experience could have lead to low-esteem and could even have caused depression if I didn't handle it well.

Coming from a community which often experiences prejudice, such as being an asylum seeker, or being poor but living in a wealthy neighbourhood, in areas where there is racial segregation or other kinds of discrimination. Individuals subjected to these prejudices and hatred can end up with low esteem.

Peer pressure to conform to social norms which you don't agree with, for example ways of dressing, lifestyles. Some kids have suffered low esteem because they are virgins or they did not take drugs. Other people have been under pressure to dress in certain labels, if one did not afford it, they feel like outsiders. In England it has been reported that most children absentee from school the days they are allowed to attend classes wearing home clothes. This is because most students feel obliged to dress in a certain way that looks appealing to their mates. However, when their parents can't afford to buy these clothes, the youngsters choose not to go to school due to peer pressure.

Bullying or excessive pressures at work- this has been explained earlier how work pressure can make one feel not good enough which triggers negative core-beliefs leading to feeling of failure and worthless.

Divorce/breakups/failure- difficult time can be detrimental to our self-esteem. If one has a divorce some people can believe they are not lovable and they are not good at relationships. I have met people who have been hurt by their previous partner and they are so angry and pessimistic about relationships. These people have sometimes turned cynical and negative towards relationships. They even end up spreading their negativity to others. For example you will hear an older woman telling younger ladies that '*all men are not trust worthy*'. That is because the person was hurt by a man years ago and hence has put all men in one jar whilst there are decent men out there. It is important if one is hurt to deal with the hurt and to try not to discourage others.

Trauma/bereavement – Death of a loved one and dealing with bereavement can be extremely difficult. I recall when my dad passed away, it was so sudden and I could not comprehend it. Unfortunately, I had just moved abroad a month earlier so I found it really hard to come to terms. I cried every night for many monthsuntil I decided to see a counsellor. The good thing is, I only went to see the person for one session and I felt better. I had to deal with my grief and tell how I felt. Some people get disorientated, depressed and lost when a loved one dies. Their identity changes and that worsen low esteem.

Physical ill-health – Illness can impact on your quality of life and engagement in different activities, hence one can loses self-identify and confidence leading to low esteem. Especially for people who loose independence, or work or a hobby they loved because of illness. Other people who have surgery and lose a body part can find it detrimental to their identity. I have come across women who had breast cancer and their breast had been removed and the change was overwhelming. Also when sports men and women have an injury and they cannot go back to their career or hobby.

Facing redundancy or being unemployed/loss of business - Indeed loss of financial and career stability can cause one to lose self-esteem because their social and individual status and lifestyles are affected.

Social isolation and loneliness- some people are unable to engage effectively in social situations. Hence this enhances low esteem. One's negative core beliefs are strengthened for example- nobody cares or you are not worth it.

During my work in mental health and counselling I have met a lot of people who suffer from low self-esteem. Some realize it in time and seek help, but others are unaware whilst others are in denial of their situation. However with great support and hard work most people have been able to turn a corner and rebuild healthy self-esteem. Although, we all feel intimidated in different situations the difference comes in how we choose to challenge those negative thoughts and core beliefs. When we decide not to be defined by our circumstances, but to rise above the storm and keep fighting for what we deserve.

Everyone in this world has potential to make it in life and to enjoy life to the maximum. We might not have similar talent, we might not all be billionaires but we can all succeed with our own spectrum and be happy about it and have healthy lifestyles. We need to know when our esteem is being attacked by our thoughts, attitudes, and beliefs or circumstances so that we can deal with it.

Signs of low self esteem
- Too sensitive to criticism by others.
- Very critical of self and others and can be a perfectionist.
- Negative/ catastrophic thinking of issues.
- Fear of mistakes leading to indecisions.
- Poor self-care and poor social interactions.
- Envious of others and can be sometimes hostile.
- Needs reassurance most of the time and very dependant.
- Unhealthy life styles with destructive behaviours like

workaholic, alcoholic, over-exercising, prostitution, overspending, isolation from social situations, self-harming etc.

- Has emotional problems, anxiety and stress disorders.
- Eating disorders - bulimic, anorexic, binge eating, obesity.

Ways of improving self esteem

1. Identify and deal effectively with negative core beliefs.

The constant negative thoughts and self-talks will drain down your confidence and self-value. Like constantly saying, 'I am a loser,' or 'no one wants me' or 'I must win, otherwise I am not good enough'. This amount of negativity will drain you down, so start to talk back to yourself positively. For example say to yourself when you feel low that 'it is okay if I win some and loose some, it is part of life'. Challenge the negative core-beliefs by stating the real facts. For example, if you feel low and unlovable because your parent did not show you real affection, then was it something you did or was it that your parent had personal issues or circumstances that led to their behaviour? Then if your parents were in difficult circumstances or having a significant problem like an addiction or an illness, then it is not you who was unlovable, it was their issues that influenced their behaviour. Hence, the truth is not that you are unlovable, but that the person you expected love from could not give it at the time and in the way you expected.

So, do not base your life on those circumstances, but on the fact that there are people around you who like or appreciate you and even love you. I have come across adults who are angry with their parents who did not show them affection when they were young. Some of these individuals even lose their marriages over the past unresolved anger. They forget that their parent's behaviour should be in past and hence they should appreciate the current or future good relationships.

If one is unable to fully challenge these negative core-beliefs on their own, they should seek professional help.

Otherwise if you go through life basing it on negative core-beliefs it will not be happy or successful. In some instances the core-beliefs can lead to negative behaviour which is detrimental to one's health and life in general. As a Christian proverb states that small foxes can spoil a nice vine yard, hence watch out for these little foxes (issues) that can spoil your vine (life).

2. Stop comparing yourself to others.

There will always be someone better than you somewhere. You might be a good singer but you will find someone else who is a good cook or a good singer and violin player. Be the best you can and appreciate your talents and commend other people's gifts. When we learn to celebrate others without jealousy and envy and also without putting ourselves down, then we will not feel intimidated. Moreover, we are able to feel confident about what we are good at and work progressively well with it.

3. Do not put yourself down. Accept your limitations and mistakes.

No one in this whole world is exempted from making mistakes in life. In fact, most millionaires became successful after becoming bankrupt a few times. I'm not suggesting that you get yourself into debt, but what I am saying is that we can choose to learn lessons from our failures and mistakes and move on. Once we move on, we should choose never to repeat the mistakes. So do not waste time crying over spilt milk, just learn how to handle the situation differently next time. You have three choices when bad things happen to you, you can let it destroy you, let it define you, or let it develop you.

I suggest you let experiences to develop you for the better.

4. Forgiveness.

This is a vital part of life and life skill we all ought to learn, nonetheless it is very difficult. In life we will be hurt by others and it might make us angry, bitter and we ruminate on it for a long time. Some offenses can take us days, years or decades to get over them because of the pain, which can lead to low esteem as a result. For example loss of marriage, business or health can be detrimental.

Once, I met an older couple who had worked so hard and succeeded in building their business. Then when their eldest daughter got married, they let the son in-law help out in the business. He did well for a few years, but with time things went from good to nasty. In the end they lost the business due to the mistakes by their son in-law just when the old couple was about retiring. The scandal was so immense hence they lost everything they had worked for many years. So, they had to start again from scratch and due to these problems they moved out of the country. Whilst abroad the couple was working shoddy jobs to earn a living. Eventually, due to the strain of life problems their daughter got separated, leaving her to take care of her children. This encounter was so detrimental to the whole family, since they had lost their business, home, status and retirement savings. They had to choose to go on living with anger or to let go of what their son in-law did.

Many of us might have never forgiven him, but this couple did. They knew carrying the burden of anger in their life was not only distressing to their present, but also to their future.

Anger and offence can cause you to have emotional and physical problems which might affect your self-value eventually. Due to feelings of betrayal one might indulge in destructive behaviors, which in the end will affect self-esteem negative. Hence, it is important for us to learn to forgive no matter how hard it seem. Especially for those who had abusive pasts or poor upbringing, forgive those who treated you unfairly and deal with the core-beliefs. Seek professional help if you need it. Remember, forgiveness does not exonerate whoever hurt you, nor does it trivialize your trauma. However, it liberates you from reliving the agonies that aren't worth your precious time and life. Offended people are not happy people, and our aim is to live a happy and healthy life. So choose in advance to forgive those who hurt you, the power is in your hands.

As Martin Luther King stated, *forgiveness is not an occasional act but it is an attitude.*

5. Get into a habit of thinking and saying positive things about yourself.

Remember, your life will always move in the direction of your strongest thought and talks. This is because your talks and thoughts influence your choices, actions and behaviour. Then, when the behaviour and actions becomes constant then your lifestyle is formed. As a result, it is paramount that you choose to think and talk positively.

If you convince yourself and others that you are a looser then you will start acting like one whilst others will start treating you like one. Subsequently, the negative self-proclamation will come to pass. I have seen a lot of people with mental health issues who believe they were not worthy to live well because of their bad past. But then again if one believes in themselves even others start to believe in them.

Just watch a football match and see how good players persuade the fans they will do it and hence they get their support. So what are you telling yourself and your supporters?

The same theory is applicable when looking for a job. Your employer must be convinced that you can deliver, but if you tell them you can't then they will get someone else who can do it. So do not talk or think yourself out of good life or success or even good self-esteem. Stay positive and affirm yourself.

6. Accept compliments and do not take criticism personally.

When we allow others and ourselves to enjoy our achievements it boosts our confidence and creativity. If someone compliments you for your dressing or for good work done, accept it. It will unconsciously bring in satisfaction to your inner self and you will be able to explore that uniqueness. Although at time some people might be sarcastic while giving their compliments, it is good to accept genuine compliments.

For example,I started a creative writing group when I worked in mental health and I felt a little bit nervous writing and sharing my ideas. However, as we continued to write, others were genuinely impressed by my writing and asked for copies of the writings. With time, I started to post my blog writings on face-book and on African Women in Europe website (A.W.E) and I got complimented and the articles raised very insightful discussions over life issues that were not usually discussed.

As I continued to accept feedback, my confidence and enjoyment for writing grew and that's how I have continued to write till now am writing this book. Still, I got criticism on my English or for my ideas. I must admit, sometimes I found it challenging but with time I consciously choose to take the criticism positively to build myself.

My experience in writing demonstrates how accepting compliment and criticism can boost you. Remember handling effectively any type of criticism is a sign of maturity and self-control. So aim to graciously and wisely accept criticism, but do not let it affect you personally. You have to know that we all see things with the eye of our personality, experience and perspective, so we have to accept others' views, if it is genuine. Then use it to build self, but not to beat yourself down.

7. Spend time with positive and supportive people.

The people you spend time with have great influence to your attitude and choices. Corresponding to what you hear empowers your thoughts, talks and action. Some of the talks can come from other people. As a result, one needs to take care of whom they associate with. In some circumstances we do not have a choice for example if it is your parents speaking negatively you have no choice until you leave home when you grow up. If it is at work, until you have another job or change the office or department. However, if it is possible to leave a toxic and negative environment I recommend it.

Certainly, you have ultimate choice whether to remain in those circumstances, especially if they are negative friends. You do not realize how negative hearing affects you until you listen to a political song for some time talking about some issue. By the time you have left the environment, the message has influenced your thinking unless challenged. That is why advertising industry thrives on repeatedly bombarding people with information, once you hear it constantly even though you dislike the product, you end up getting close to it.

The same happens when you hang around negative crowds, eventually they will affect you. That is why it is important for a person recovering from an addiction to abstain from people indulging with the same behavior they are trying to overcome. Equivalent effort should be taken to enhance self-esteem, indulge with people who builds your esteem or people with good esteem. Break free from dysfunctional associations.

8. Acknowledge your positives qualities and engage in them.

Knowing your talents, abilities and using your opportunities healthily, will not only help in your progress and success, but will also aid your esteem. Some of the qualities you have could be creativity, accounts, writing, counselling, teaching or caring for others. If you enjoy doing one of these things, then take opportunities where you can engage in them. You may also choose a career path in the line of your talent and passion and then you will not only enjoy the path but also excel in it.

If you are good at interacting and communicating with others, then you can do sales and marketing, if you choose a career behind the desk where you rarely speak, then you will feel low by the end of the day. I have seen some bosses spending most of their time outside their office to engage with others in the departments while derailing (falling behind?) on their paper work. These individuals could be more suited in jobs where they engage with people face to face.

Other people who are introverts might love working alone, hence they should enjoy doing things like IT consultants or computer programming, or accounting or creative arts where they engage with figures or computers or nature and less with other people. Every ability, talent and quality is profitable if used appropriately, we should enjoy our uniqueness and maximize our potential.

9. Be assertive, do not allow disrespect.

As I mentioned earlier, bullying and work pressure are great causes of low esteem. Hence, if we allow our friends, colleagues or mates treat us with disrespect then we are damaging our esteem. We need to lay boundaries in our relationships, to let others know when they cross the line. This protects our emotions from getting hurt and also others from hurting you unconsciously.

More on relationships will be discussed in another chapter but it is important to resolve issues in relationships especially when you feel disrespected. Fear of losing the relationship or fear of being considered a bad person can stop us. However, if you let other people disrespect you, their actions will be detrimental to your esteem.

Communicate your feelings to them, how their behavior make you feel. When we communicate we make the other person know the repercussions of their behaviour and we hope they can change. If the behaviour persists then you can choose to cut off the relationship. It is also vital for you to reflect whether your fears of addressing the issue are due to negative core-beliefs. Hence, address negative core-beliefs and face up assertively to your relationships with others.

For example most women in abusive relationships allow a dominant spouse to disrespect them through verbal aggression and insults. Some of the reasons they do not address the issues are because they somehow believe they deserve to be treated that way. Research has shown that most women in abusive relationships came from dysfunctional background (Illinois 2011, Ellen et al 2003). Hence, their expectation and experiences in childhood lead to them allowing others to disrespect them.

It is never late to address negative core-beliefs and also to discontinue abusive relationships. Now is the time to make healthy choices by not allowing others to disrespect you.

10. Be helpful to other people.

There is great boost of self-confidence when we help other people. No matter where you are in life there is always someone who is worse off than you in one area of life and they can do with your help. Your skills, experiences and knowledge that can help someone, so why not spend some quality time impacting someone else's life. This will help you reduce time for negative thinking and self-pity, and it will give you time to explore on the good things you have.

Some people are good at baking and they can use their skills to bake cakes for some children in a care home. Maybe your IT technical skills can help some students struggling with their projects or slow laptops. Overall, while you are impacting others, you will be surprised that you will also be building relationships. Moreover, the sense of achievement will create feeling of happiness enhancing your esteem.

Most people, women and teenagers especially, spend a lot of time looking in the mirror finding faults on their figures, the big nose that they dislike, but this time can be spent mentoring others or helping out in their community. Then, the feeling of low esteem will be zapped out. I challenge you to practice giving little acts of kindness like by being nice and helpful to people you meet daily at school or at work or in your neighborhood. Kindness bounces backs once we give to others generously, it also boosts one's self-esteem.

11. Engage in activities that you enjoy.

One of my family recollections is the differences between the siblings. My brother Nash, even at a very young age could dismantle our radio and reconstruct it. Of course, when my mother found her radio in pieces it drove her mad, but within a few hours her radio was working as good as new. Nowadays, Nash is an electrician running his own business.

I, on the other hand, had no interest in practical work of fixing and assembling, but to tell you the truth I had no capability. Nevertheless, I remember growing up in the farm and our parents during school holidays gave us two choices on how to spend our time, it was either by helping in the farm work or reading our school books. Guess what I choose? I choose to read my books. It doesn't mean I was a good scholar, but at the time it was escapism from farm work, but eventually I have become a scholar all my life. I have realized I enjoy reading, studying and writing. Conversely, if my parents insisted that we all do the same things, it could have lowered our esteem in engaging in activities that we are not good at. Hence, it is important for individuals to uphold engagements in activities they do well in.

Oh, and I will not forget to voice out that my youngest brother Pat is a good keyboard player. He was even was once asked to play for the president of Kenya when he visited our hometown. And guess what? Nobody else in our nuclear family can sing or play an instrument. But he chose to follow his passion and has excelled in it and sometimes he teaches others in the county to play keyboard. Overall, our distinct qualities and interests are diverse, but when appreciated and put into practice, we excel, boosting our self-esteem and life pleasure.

12. Get help for persistent destructive behavior.

Destructive habits and lifestyles can be hard to get over for example alcoholism, drug addiction, gambling. There are other habits that derail our success, health and happiness, for example excessive buying which leaves us in debt, habits like negative thinking and talking, bad company, breaking the law or not telling the truth to others.

At first, these behaviours are fun and seems harmless, but the more they become habitual, they start damaging our lives. For example one might take a glass of wine once a week and it is okay for relaxation and as others suggest good for digestion. Then the person starts to take twice a week and then a glass every night. Then, it moves to two glasses when one feels sad or tired and within a few years the individual is taking a bottle every evening. With time the individual can't sleep or go to work or face stressful situations without a drink. In UK where alcohol consumption is acceptable for social engagements like having a glass after work in a local pub or during weekend parties, the country have ended up with so many cases of people becoming alcohol dependent.

The effect of alcohol addiction has caused the UK government a lot of millions of pounds every year dealing with the repercussions. On the other side, most people have lost their jobs, marriages, families and even died as a result of this conventional habit by the society. According to Alcohol Concern UK website, I.6 million people were reported to be alcohol dependent in 2011 and 8748 people died due to alcohol related problems. Furthermore, it was estimated that 2.6 million children in the UK are living with parents who are drinking hazardously and 705,000 of them are living with dependent drinkers. Alcohol is also reported to be a casual problem of more than 60 medical conditions including liver problems, high blood pressure and depression (Alcohol Concern UK). This is very sad and we all need to learn from it.

Overall, alcohol problems are not the only destructive habits around us. We need to be aware of these habits in our lives and seek help before they destroy us. Most people have destroyed their careers, relationships and eventually their health through these destructive habits. If you know something that is not helpful don't try it, observe from others lessons and walk away. If you got yourself into them already try and get out or seek help. For example, if you find you are always above your budget stop the impulse buying, carry enough cash for your daily needs. It is better to deal with the problems head on, than the consequences when it is too late.

If you are in a bad relationship, deal with it sooner than later.

13. Use self-help books and websites to help change your negative beliefs.

Seeking to learn skills is a good way to succeed in upholding good self-esteem. There are different ways of addressing different situations that we face in our lives, whilst maintaining good self-image throughout our lifespan. If we lose our self in the day to day agendas and not pay attention to how we feel, we become our own enemy.

Most cultures across the world pays less attention to inner feelings, however ignoring how we feel doesn't make the feelings go away. We just repress and suppress them but they unconsciously affect our behavior. As a result, the rate of unprecedented suicides and mental health problems heightens in these cultures. So, it is vital to get a good book or visit a good website and learn more how to deal with issues positively. I am even more glad that you are already doing it by reading this book, keep up and advice others to do so.

14. Enjoy your achievements and work towards current life goals confidently.

We all work so hard and sometimes we rarely compliment ourselves. If others do not do it for you, do it for yourself. In fact, when you have a goal in life and you are working towards it, make sure you have also written down to reward yourself once you achieve your goal.

Acknowledge the success of your hard work no matter how insignificant it might seem. It lifts your motivation and self-esteem. No matter how small the step is towards the right direction, be grateful for it. For example, if John was struggling with self-control and was getting into fights when angry and is now working on anger management. When he then gets frustrated and is able to keep his mouth shut, he should celebrate his progress.

Another person maybe named Jack might argue that he has never got into fights hence there is no need to celebrate. However this is a great achievement is John's who has anger issues but not James. So, like John celebrate your achievements no matter how small they seem. If you were struggling with negative thoughts in the past and now you are less self-critical, then celebrate with a piece of cake. If having a tasking project at work, have a break and treat yourself with a movie night or go on holiday after a long semester.

Plan and do things that celebrate your achievements. You can also take time to ask those who supported you through the season to celebrate with you. The enjoyment will not only build your emotional health back but also your physical health too, boosting your esteem as well. Most of us rarely stop to celebrate but we expect others to do it for us. But it is within our power to show them the way to celebrate our success.

15. Seek and accept friendly or professional help during stressful seasons in your life.

In life we all go through disappointments and setbacks that we cannot comprehend. Perhaps, if you are a believer you prayed for a loved one, but they didn't get well. Or maybe you worked hard for a promotion, but you didn't get it. You worked hard for a relationship, but it didn't work out. One of the best things you can do is release it. Let it go. Don't dwell on it anymore.

If you go around wondering why things didn't work out, you will end up bitter, resentful and floating in self-pity. Before long, you'll be blaming others, blaming yourself, or even God. It may not have been fair, but when you discharge it and start re-building back your life. You will gain energy and health for the future days coming ahead. I believe you still have something good in future and you should not shy away from asking for help when you can't manage on your own.

Do not be like the lady I mentioned in my first chapter who was struggling with the child's buggy but didn't accept help. Most of us have life 'buggies' that are detrimental to our lives but we do not let go of them. Nevertheless, if we did let go we would have successful, healthy and happier lives. So, we need to seek help when we have failed to do it on our own. In simple matters, we can ask a helping hand from a friend or a caring colleague or neighbor.

Remember we all need another at times and no one is perfect. I have seen some mothers doing a good job in their motherhood role, however due to the hassle of life they are left physically and emotionally drained. Since they rarely had time to re-energize and they did not ask for support. I encourage you to ask for help from those around you if they are able to help. I know they will be happy to do it. If you are a Christian like me pray God to help. Most people have argued that faith is a clutch but if you have been a believer you would know the power of prayer and faith in God.

Even so, some life problems like bereavement, divorce, debt and illnesses can be detrimental to our lives leaving us feeling helpless and with low esteem. Those around us can also be challenged in assisting in these circumstances. Sometimes, even though you are praying you can still requisite professional help. In the same way you take syrup medicine for a cold or flu, seek psychological support for self-esteem issues. For example if you had an insecure childhood or abusive relationships or traumatic incidents which might have left you with negative core-beliefs you are struggling to overcome, seek professional help. There are therapists, psychologists or even doctors and counselors out there ready to help you. It breaks my heart to see people go a through life affected by psychological issues which can be addressed and supported by professionals.

Please seek help, you will only feel vulnerable initially, but professionals are trained to help you and they do want to help, but you have to let them. Seek their help when hit with hard life issues and remember the key to success is to let go of fear and deal with issues promptly and effectively.

16. Parents support and give positive affirmations to your children.

As explained by most psychologists and therapists, most mental health issues especially those related to esteem are triggered by problematic upbringing. They can be as a result of insecure attachments or due to parental divorce or death of a loved one or separation from a care-giver. Still, some children are born with health conditions and disabilities which are problematic in their childhood. Hence, it is important for the care-givers and parents and all those who come in contact with the children to affirm them whilst they are young. I have seen children with challenging disability become world champions, just because their parents taught them to believe they can. When children know that their parents love them and do not treat them differently, they endeavor to achieve.

Currently, most young people have distorted self-images due to peer-pressure and media influence of who they should be and the body size they should have. No wonder most young people have low esteem and are suffering from eating disorders and anxiety problems among other mental and physical health issues. Parents, if you do not tell your children how worthy and valued they are, someone else will tell them whom they are and what they are not.

Help your children to build healthy esteem through positive affirmations. Do not push your children to heights they cannot reach, to fulfil your failed dreams or your own ego. Accept their abilities, gifts, talents and also their failures. This habit should also be extended to the other family members and also to spouses for better relationships and healthier self-esteem of individuals.

Here are ways of knowing if you have a healthy self-esteem.

- Accepts self and less judgmental of self and others.
- Gets along with others easily.
- Resists manipulation and works with others in healthy collaborations.
- Takes care of self and has life goals.
- Accepts mistakes and setbacks in life, deals with them and moves on.
- Doesn't need constant reassurance of others to maintain self-confidence.
- Less competitive with others and maintains a balanced lifestyle.
- Celebrates life achievement for self and others.
- Maintains positive affirmations, attitudes, thoughts and behaviour most of the time.

Generally, a person with low esteem can learn to overcome it, through self-help or professional help by a counsellor or a therapist or a psychologist. So, do not give up if you have low self-esteem, learn and work at it. Sometime in life, especially when undergoing through difficult times we all need to boost our esteem constantly, through use of positive affirmations or good association. We need to do this consciously at first, until it becomes a way of life especially for people who have grown up in negative environment where they were criticised constantly. You can learn the walk of boosting your self-confidence. Never give up, keep practicing the skills specified in this book.

ii)MANAGING ANGER

One winter afternoon as I waited for a bus to go home after a long day at work, I stood next to a big family. The family comprised of a couple (father and mother), with five kids between ages of 3 years to 10 years old. I could not stop myself noticing that two of their children were beautiful twin girls who were happily playing with each other. They appeared to be of about 6 years of age. Their older brother teased them from a distance. I enjoyed the view of the family, especially since am not used to see big families standing at the bus stops. Most of young families with bigger numbers prefer to have cars for easier travels. So I was thinking quietly.

Suddenly, as the kids played with each other, the dad shouted at them ' stop, stop playing stop!!'. The kids were terrified by the dad's uncalled for exclamation. I also couldn't wait for my bus to come so that I could leave the situation. The anger outburst of this man changed the environment from happiness to fear and anxiety for all at the bus stop. I wondered if the anger outburst was underlying or was it just about the kids' playful behaviour?

Anger is an emotion we feel when things do not go as we mentally anticipated. Mostly, when we feel some one wronged us or disappointed us or we failed at a particular task. Anger can be towards circumstances, others or towards self. When one is offended the anger can move from feeling uncomfortable to being very angry and then one can have a reaction. Hence, angers starts with a mental interpretation of the situation and then the person responds biologically by sweating, feeling agitated and then a reaction through behaviour can be projected. Behaviour can be voicing frustration, crying or getting into an outburst or shouting out the frustration.

The process of anger is dissimilar to different people according to their perception and values regarding different circumstances. A good example is how one person can feel if a certain phrase is used in a conversation. The person who perceived the phase to be demeaning they might get irritated about it. If the phrase is continually used, then the agitated person might get aggressive and verbally or physically react toward the perceived assailant. Nonetheless, another person in the conversation who might not understand or perceive the phase as insulting might be surprised by the aggression of the person who reacted.

The perception might be shaped by previous encounters or experiences. Hence, despite the intention of the phase, the historical knowledge might shape the reaction. If the victim had knowledge of the perpetrator as a good person they might tolerate them, however if they might have knowledge of them being bad in the past the tolerance level may be limited. Sometimes, historical knowledge would be related to other issues like political or social economic issues. If the person perceives the other person as unfair historically or as an enemy, then the anger can easily escalate.

Having lived in multicultural society, I have witnessed bounty of repressed and suppressed anger among different people, which comes out on unrelated issues. However, when you dig deep, the cause of anger was historically based for example, the empathies of world war I & II in the 19th century, like the relations between Germans and Jews or the African American Black history. This historical based anger can sometimes erupt in football grounds, or in schools or in social settings when one group distinguishes the other as atrocious and they draw their sensitivity from history not current issues.

Another influence of our perspective would be the embodied situation which means our current circumstances can influence how we perceive a situation. Indeed, one's state of mind might influence their reactions and thoughts towards the situation for example, one might be tired or in a bad mood, or going through a rough patch in their personal life. Hence, the person's reaction might be different to the circumstances on a good day. Still, a person's expectations can lead to anger emotion for example if one expected to pass an exam or be interviewed for a promotion, the frustration of not getting what they wanted can lead to anger emotion towards self or others.

Feelings of anger are normal and everyone at some point will be angry and frustrated by something. Even so, our reaction during anger emotion is the difference. Someone might decide to leave the situation instead of becoming verbally aggressive. Another person might become aggressive and insult or even assault. Hence, how we manage anger is paramount. At the same time, how often one gets angry and reacts might make a difference. I believe all of us have been angry at some point and reacted to the situation maybe by shouting or crying or running away from the situation or you got caught up in a fight.

If you go through your life honestly you might have been in such a situation. However, I believe if it is once or twice in a lifetime it's normal. However if it is every week or daily then it gets alarming. The habit or behaviour can make you feel helpless and agitated most of the time and can leave others fearful of you and make them avoid you. The behaviour is not attractive in any relationships whether romantic, family or work relationship.

Types of Anger:

1.Productive Anger- As noted above, when you lose control you risk losing other things as well, like the respect of others or the chance to find a constructive solution. Productive anger is the annoyance which pushes one to address issues appropriately which might be inflicting pain or injustice to self or others. For example anger towards human suffering is not only appropriate but it is the catalyst for change. Also, if an individual feels they are not respected or others are subjected to unfair treatment, the person would voice their views effectively in a way to find change or solution. The means of addressing the issue should not be aggressive but appropriately, direct and solution based.

A good example is when colleagues feel their work rota is not well balance. The person needs to voice the concerns to the person who does the rota to get an explanation and then reach to a solution. If they agree on the solution then the issue is gone and the anger will subsidise. However, if the person is not ready to understand, this might lead to the situation escalating. However, by moving the case to the next person in leadership would be appropriate.

2. Passive anger- This is the type of anger which is suppressed by the individual however it is not full dealt with. The person might be boiling on the inside but they might be trying to cover it up and appear cool about things. However, this type of anger still comes out in other passive ways. For example the person might use sly comments to hit back to the person they feel angered them. Taking our previous example of a worker who is angry with the roster plan, he/she might not address the situation but cunningly be sarcastic toward the roster planner whenever they come in contact. The culprit might take the passive aggression higher by spreading negative rumours about the roster planner in the place of work.

Types of people who displays passive aggression;

A. Somatizer- The person sits on top of your anger but don't let it out. The person lets the emotions become toxic in the brain and body chemistry hence can suffer from migraine headaches, ulcers or high blood pressure. These are the kind of that are people pleasers hence they avoid hurting others' feelings when they suffer in silence. However, they can choose to cut off all communication with the person they perceive as the offender.

B. Self-punisher- One can turn their anger into negative talk about themselves. Some can self-punish through self-harming which includes cutting themselves, drinking alcohol, starving themselves, punching and hitting things that hurt them like brick walls. They generally make themselves comfortable with it being their own fault that they were offended. Often feel they are not worth respect.

C. Under-handers- The individual doesn't want to expose themselves to others by exploding because then they would have to take responsibility for their actions. Hence they retaliate by using back stabbing remarks and getting one's own back, which they feel is a fair game. The person isolates themselves. They can react toward the perceived 'enemy' through actions like door slamming and sarcasm. Sometime their aggression can also be rated as passive aggression.

3. Aggressive anger- Is when an individual's anger is high and boiling and they lose control of self and react aggressively towards others or self. Some people can assault others or violently attack others using weapons whilst other can self-harm. If this kind of anger is not subsided immediately the aggression can rise and cause major harm to self or others. Some people have been injured in an angry attack which started off as harmless. This is very frequently in bars when people are intoxicated and their rate of patience is deterred or their judgment and self-control is distorted by the alcohol. But if one is in a habit of getting into anger outburst this behaviour is beyond the situation but might be triggered by inner emotion of frustration and aggression. There are people who are aggressive and they tend to blame other people or their circumstance. However, each individual has responsibility to manage anger emotion rationally.

The types of people who display aggressive anger;

A.Exploder-The person openly lets the distress out. Although, anger emotions are normal emotion, when exploding the aggression can be unreasonable and quite disruptive. Sometimes, the person receiving the anger outburst is not necessarily the one that created the reason for the anger. A good example is when a mother is angry with the husband and the children seem to be on the receiving end. Hence the explosion is unreasonable and not proportionate, neither healthy for the children since they might be frightened or feel unloved or confused by the explosion.

How to deal with Anger Emotions:

BREATHING AND RELAXATION TECHNIQUES

Most therapists have used this technique to help clients to learn how to calm down in heated situation or in times of stress, anxiety and anger. One need to consciously have deep breathes in and out simultaneously for a while until they feel calmer. The deep breathing helps your mind to focus on something else apart from the anger situation. It also allows your body to cool off since anger emotions makes one's adrenaline high and the body gets hot and tenses. One can also try to count number from 1-100. This will also help you calm down.

Also relaxation use of different methods like listening to calm and cool music in a comfortable room can be helpful for anger to subside. Likewise engaging in an activity that you enjoy like drawing, baking or watching a movie or engaging in an exercise like swimming playing tennis can help you relax and diminish anger feelings.

TAKE TIME OUT

When feelings of Anger overwhelm you in a social situation, it is important to try and take control of your feelings. Sometime, in the heat of a moment if we allow our anger to take control we can say or do things we can't take back and hurt self or others, for example, at work with colleagues or at home with family and friends. Hence, in social setting, it is helpful if you feel your anger is rising up to get out of the room and have time to cool off. Move away from the environment that is anger provoking and remove any cues that enhance anger.

AVOID ARGUEMENTS

Do you sometimes find yourself saying, 'I get so angry when they refuse to listen to my viewpoint? How can I make them listen and hear what I'm trying to say?'

Unless you're involved in an official debate, arguing with someone who's unwilling to listen is useless and a waste of time. State your viewpoint with clarity and purpose, but don't become defensive and argumentative if it's not received.

You'll only hurt yourself and the relationship if you become argumentative. Don't allow anyone to draw you into strife or arguing. Hold your tongue, and try to remember these words of wisdom in Proverbs: 'A gentle anger turns away wrath, but a harsh word stirs up anger,' 'The tongue of the wise makes knowledge acceptable, but the mouth of a fool spurts folly.'

RESOLVE CONFLICTS

Conflict resolution is part of anger and stress management. When you learn to address issues in a mature manner then you will be able to control your feeling of anger and frustration. If you feel you are unfairly treated do not suppress the issues otherwise you might start being passive aggressive and when one day you reach breaking point you might end up being aggressive. Hence, seek to speak to the person and tell them how their behaviour makes you feel. Then listen to their side of view and seek to have a resolution. If they listen and agree to work with you towards the solution then follow up with actions and review the process.

STOP THE BLAME GAME

Blaming creates enemies, when you blame others for your anger and behaviour. The person you are blaming will ignore you, compile numerous proofs of their innocence, and resent you. Their friends will defend them and become your enemies. Even your own friends will get fed up with your complaining and distance you. When the blame game becomes a way of life, the person is in denial of their feelings and behaviour, however they hurt themselves and the relationships they have with other people. The person who justifies everything they do by blaming others, in the end they hurt themselves.

It is important for one to face their feelings and be ready to deal with them. It is crucial for you to identify the addiction to blaming others, and then to give up the blame game. Own responsibility for your life and take back your power to respond to things accordingly.

LET GO OF OFFENSES

One of the rules of life given Colin Powell's book the former USA secretary of state was "Get mad and Get over it quick". Indeed, anger is an emotion we all experience, but what you do with it make the difference. For you to be free emotionally, spiritually and even physically productive in life you need to learn to let go of offenses. At times it is hard to do, when you feel very offended. Nonetheless, you will be doing yourself a favour more than the person/s you are forgiving.

Unforgiving can lead to physical illnesses like headaches, ulcers, depression, eating & emotional disorders. Relationships get damaged and one finds it difficult to form healthy relationships later in life. Some people's dysfunctional lifestyles and behaviour and also mental illnesses have been triggered by trauma, anger and lack of forgiveness.

It's high time we overcome the blame game and take responsibility. Your maturity depends on your willingness to face issues, forgive and forget the past.

Do not poison your future with the pain of past failures or bad experiences or anger, let go!

Mahatma Gandhi said 'The weak can never forgive. Forgiveness is the attribute of the strong.'

DEAL WITH PERSONAL ISSUES

Some outbursts and recurring anger issues can be caused by underlying psychological and emotional problems which have not been dealt with. We respond in different ways to anger and when we are aware of how we respond, and then we can identify repressed anger emotions and deal with issues which have caused the anger. Also acknowledging our feeling of anger and frustration on certain matters is the first step to progress. Thereafter, address the issues or seek help from friends and family or from a profession which could be a counsellor, a therapist or psychologists. I have seen adults who grew up with feeling of anger towards their parents and they never addressed the issue. Nonetheless, the hidden anger regresses their progress on building trustful relationships or on their mental and physical health. So it is important to seek guidance and counselling when you realise you have anger feeling that are predominant in your life.

It is not healthy or joyful to carry with you a burden of anger. You can succeed in your career but if you are constantly angry, others might find it difficult to work around you and hence you might feel isolated and unloved. Seek help and deal with anger issues effectively.

Overall, being able to deal with anger problems in your life effectively is a vital aspect of life skill that will help you manage your stress level. It also helps you be able to build relationships and also be able to solve conflicts appropriately. Subsequently, you will be mentally and physically healthier. People who have recurring anger issues end up suffering from different mental health issues like depression and also they have social issues like isolation and broken relationships. If one is constantly angry their physical body also suffers from ailments like ulcers and anxiety disorders. Once you manage your anger you are happier, healthier and have energy to focus on your goals and you have the potential to succeed.

iii) HANDLING DEPRESSION

Gail my college mate whose name is changed for anonymity was a very beautiful and intelligent girl. She came from a wealthy background but was humble enough to associate with all. In college Gail seemed to have it all, she was doing well in her academics, she was beautiful and rich. She also had a great boyfriend who took her and her friends out during the weekends. On Monday mornings, we all wanted to hear stories of their weekend adventures. Gail's life seemed to be every college girl's dream.

After a few months, it all changed when Gail broke up with her boyfriend and he went on to date her best friend. Gail was devastated and cried all the times. She became isolated and skipped a lot of classes. We all tried our best to support her, but it was close to our final exams hence we didn't have much time for her. Gail became very low in mood and one evening she attempted to commit suicide. She was taken to hospital where her parents came to see her. Her parents were very disappointed and told her off. They felt let down and insisted that she should get herself together. Gail's parents' reaction made her more depressed. I remember the time we went to see her in the hospital. She couldn't even recognise any of us, she looked very confused and depressed. Unfortunately, a few days after our visit we were informed that had Gail passed away. The news was heart breaking for all of us and left us feeling helpless. The misfortune and depression took away a young girl with a lot of potential.

Some people think depression is just a feeling of low mood, but it is more than that. Depression is a serious mental illness which requires medical attention. Depression can be mild, moderate or severe. Chronic depression can lead to suicide ideations, hence it is vital to address the problem promptly.

Statistics shows that **1 in 5** people will suffer depression at one point in their life, which is **20%** of population. **Women are likely to suffer twice more** than men. While **young adults** are sufferers too, especially among students depression was reported to be **21%** in 2011 (NCHA).

When you feel constantly low in mood and it starts to interfere with your daily life, it is then advisable to see your doctor for support and advice. Depression can make normal chores become extremely harder to do. Sometimes, due to **social stigma** towards mental health illness which includes depression, most people try to sweep the signs and symptoms under the carpet. The conduct can only makes things worse. Sometimes when people go to the doctor and are advice to seek counselling because of depression, they decline to do so because they are afraid of stigma. Intermittently people are in denial, hence they refuse to acknowledge their circumstance. However, one can only overcome what they are ready to face.

Depression can originate from various states which have been discussed earlier in this chapter. For example it can be as a result of genetic predisposition by one's parents, especially for the chronic depression for example **bipolar**

or manic depression. However, one may be genetically predisposed with the genes but can live normally under the right conditions which do not provoke stress or the illness.

On the other hand, lifestyles can trigger depression. If one is overly stressed at work or at home, the feelings of being rushed around and feeling inadequate to solve various problems can trigger depression. At the same times, life predicaments can lead to depression for example loss of a loved one or loss of a job or a business. Divorce and separation can also lead to depression. At the same times, use of illegal drugs can trigger **depressive mood disorders** or episodes of **manic depression or psychotic major depression.** If the addiction continues, one can have irreversible depression due to chemical changes in the brain.

Traumatic experiences and exposure to volatile environment can also trigger depression. The traumatic incidents for example car accidents, a major fall or working in a war zone environment leaves the person with intense memories of the episodes. The person finds it difficult to engage with others, or to concentrate or even to sleep. This is due to **Post traumatic stress disorder**(PTSD) and when one feels loss of control of their feeling and thoughts, they might end up depressed.

Some women can suffer from **post natal depression** after they have given birth. The overwhelming feelings of having a baby and the need to be a good mother can cause immense stress which leads to depression for some mothers. They can start to isolate or to have poor self-care or they can resent the baby. They feel that, the baby has immensely changed their life especially for single mothers or lone parent or even for working mums who have to juggle work and children. Another kind of mum who might find it overwhelming is a mum who was working prior to having the baby and now they have decided to be a 'stay home mum'. The drastic change can be too much for the person, especially when the individual is also suffering from low self-esteem due to increased or loss of weight during pregnancy.

Other people have suffered seasonal depression. This can be due seasonal changes in their lives or weather changes which sometime can be extreme in some parts of the world. If the season like winter makes it difficult for the person to socialise or to move around or if it comes with low business or heightened financial implications the person can suffer from **seasonal depression.**

Many people have suffered from depression and been treated. Others have been able to have successful lives despite struggling with depression in their lives at some point or throughout. For example a few high profile people, including President Abraham Lincoln, Writer J.K. Rowlings, Prime Minister Winston Churchill among others have been very successful in their chosen professions.

Having depression is not the end of life, one can manage the illness effectively and be successful, healthier and happy.

TYPES OF DEPRESSION

There are various types of depression which are clinically diagnosed. However, in this book I will not dwell fully on them, I will just mention them for your knowledge and some have been outlined in brief above. More information can be obtained from clinical books or from doctors working in mental health.

Main types of depression: - **Manic depression or bipolar disorder, postpartum depression, psychotic major depression, unipolar depression.**

Others names are -atypical depression, melancholic depression, catatonic depression, seasonal depression (SAD), paediatric depression (children, adolescents).

Signs of depression:-

- Loss of interest in daily activities like work, social engagements, relationships and sex.
- Feelings of low mood and isolation, self-neglect, guilt and withdrawal.
- Crying a lot, feelings of sadness, low self-esteem, negative thoughts, irritability.
- Harmful behaviours like heavy drinking of alcohol, drugs, gambling and self- harm.

- Overeating, oversleeping, insomnia, anxiety problems/ disorders.
- Extreme sensitivity to misunderstanding, rejection, changes.
- Physical pains without physical causes- fatigue, headaches, digestive problems.
- Low concentration, poor memory, agitation.
- Helplessness, hopelessness, suicidal ideas.
- Psychosis symptoms-delusions and hallucinations.

When you or someone you know has above presentations repeatedly, it warrants concern.It is important to acknowledge the signs of depression and seek help. One can have several signs dependant in their embodied circumstances and their mental state. As a result, it will be crucial to identify what kind of environment triggers the depression symptoms.

For example, as I worked in a rehabilitation ward I met a patient whom I will call Jane who was suffered depression from time to time. Jane would be very productive in her community and she had attained a degree in teaching and was able to get good jobs within her community. She managed her depression with support of her care team and supportive family members. However, just like any other young woman, Jane could fall in love and get into a love relationship. Conversely, she found it difficult to cope with the strains that come with relationships, so she could relapse and stop taking care of self, eventually lose her job. Sometimes, it got so bad that she had manic episodes and had to be re-admitted in a mental hospital.

So where did Jane go wrong? First, she did not identify the triggers for her condition, which was the stress of love relationships. Secondly, when the signs showed up, Jane was in denial so she did not reach out for help until it was too late, when she became unaware of her erratic behaviour.

Many people like Jane might not pay attention to triggers and signs, but if they do they can get skills and support and then continue to function normally in their environment.

How to handle depression:

Healthy lifestyles

Having healthy lifestyle is vital to mental and physical health. When you have balanced diet meals regularly gives you the right nutrients required by your body to fight stress hormones and to give you energy. Regular exercise also help with stress reduction, hence depression is reduced. One is also able to go out and socialise, reducing isolation and also increasing self-esteem.

Good positive associations, and engaging in relaxing hobbies and maintain a good 8 hours sleep will also help you overcome depression. This will be covered in the next chapter on Physical health.

Challenge negative thoughts and actively use positive self-talk

Most depressed people have low self-esteem and constantly think and talk negatively. They have a negative outlook on life, self and others. However, it helps if one gets into a habit of challenging negative thinking and try to think and talk positively.

It would be hard at first, however by listening to positive music, encouraging talks, CD's and motivation speakers regularly one can learn. Also try to write down notes with positive affirmations and pin it on your wall and read them regularly when you feel low.

Taking Control of your mind and your life

You've got the power to choose what to listen to and what to pay attention to. That is to choose what you think about and what you expose your mind to and how you spend your time. Most times we are fed with information on the news, tv, radio , computer and by other people that pollute our minds and also material that brings discouragement and loss of hope. The brain and the mind control our thoughts, feelings, talks, behaviour and eventually our lifestyles. We should take care of the information we feed to our minds just like we take care of the foods we eat.

Have you ever tried to stay away from news, newspapers or negative people for a week? It's a new good Challenge for you... STAY AWAY FROM NEGATIVE NEWS FOR A WEEK AND TAKE CONTROL OF WHAT YOU FEED YOUR MIND WITH!!

Try to switch off from your normal channels on TV and radio. Listen to an inspiring CD or DVD or take time to read a book that helps your mind stay positive, strong and hopeful. Associate with people who believe it is possible to succeed and be happy and stay away from dream killers. Take your time to pray if you do pray and also take time to reflect, refresh and cool down...You will be surprised how positive, energetic and healthy you will become. Try once in a while TAKING CONTROL OF YOUR MIND!

Getting support during traumatic periods

As identified earlier traumatic incidents or circumstances can lead to depression. They could be divorce, redundancy, grief or financial crisis. However, seeking support from family and friends who understands would be very helpful. Some people isolate when going through tough seasons, only to come back and report they were depressed the last few months or years whilst there were people who could have been there for them.

Please seek support when you need it, next time you will be their shoulder to cry on. Problems and setbacks come to everyone that is why it is important to support each other. It can be as little as distracting one another and watch a movie together, which reduces time of isolation.

Asking for professional help

GP's, psychotherapists, counsellors, psychologists, psychiatrists, social workers and other mental health professionals are well trained in dealing with mental health issues and work as professionals. Therefore, they are non-judgemental, give confidential support and they have a caring heart which will reach out for you. However, as I studied in counselling you cannot help someone who is not ready to accept your help. Hence it is important for an individual to come to the point they seek help in crisis and be ready to work through. We all want to live healthy and happier lives so never shy off from asking for help. Remember when you struggled in school with chemistry or Calculus in mathematics lesson. What did you do? You asked the teacher to help you so that you can pass your exams. Same to real life now, ask for help if you are struggling with depression so that you can succeed in all areas of your life. Do not give up, do what it takes to attain good mental health for a happier and successful life.

Use of prescribed anti-depressant medication

There are various prescriptions that help with depression but it is important if they are prescribed by a qualified doctor or a psychiatrist. Hence, I will not recommend any prescription since I am not a doctor but a therapist. However I believe that anti-depressant medication is good for chemical balance and all biological work it does, however when combined with good lifestyle and therapy it is most beneficial. Some of the medication have side effects like increase of appetite, mood swings among others but can be reduced if you get advice from your doctor. I have met several patients in my work experience, who take prescribed medication for some time and when they stabilise they stop taking them, without doctor's advice. This behaviour sets them up for a relapse, which is at times even worse than the previous episode. Stopping or reducing intake of medication is done gradually to maintain chemical balance and drastic change can be very unhelpful especially for people who suffer bipolar disorder or manic depression. Hence, it is important for one to seek doctor's advice before stopping the medication despite the side effects or the persons view on their mental wellness. I have met some individuals' in the church who decided to stop medication because they prayed for it. From my experience I would be very cautious on that and recommend doctor's advice.

Finally on psychological wellbeing: It is everyone's responsibility to identify people around them who have mental health issues and **support** them. It could be your family, neighbour, workmate or a friend. Some issues cannot be resolved by prayer and love alone, however. Practical and professional intervention is crucial. If it is beyond you, then advise the person to seek help via available support services. Good news is, depression and most mental health illnesses can be treated. If you are the one suffering please **take the advice** above and do the right thing for you and for the sake of the people who love you. As statistics shows more than 20% of population will have mental health issues in their life time (NHCA 2011). This could be long term issues or short time episodes. Nonetheless, one can get through these times with good support and still be productive in their lives. Hence we need to **reduce the stigma** around mental health issues.

As identified in this chapter, they can be as a result of biological dispositions or chemical imbalances or they can be triggered by traumatic experiences in life, which we are all prone to. Hence, there is no need to point fingers and blames others. It would be beneficial to support one another, understand their predicament and overcome our prejudices. Give similar sympathy you do to cancer patients or other patients of physical illnesses. Nobody would like to have any kind of illness, so it would make it easier if we are all more supportive and sympathetic. This would reduce the rates of people suffering with mental health issues hiding and giving up in life or feeling worthless and as failures.

Acceptance and understanding would help individuals to seek help. **All of us need to take care of our psychological, emotional and mental health**. Without good mental health, productivity is challenged, so try and look after your anger emotions management, boosting a healthy self-esteem and promptly deal with issues that depress you easily. Then you will experience health and happiness as you walk the road to happiness effortlessly.

CHAPTER 2 :GOOD PHYSICAL HEALTH

Occasionally, I feel like we all have enough information on physical health through our academic studies in school and the media commercials and also all the information given by our doctors and leaflets available in our hospitals and community centres. Nevertheless, it is important to have constant reminders on how to take care of our bodies. Indeed, my reservations on our intense knowledge are challenged by the rate of increased physical diseases and ailments in our society. So am obligated to go through them again, since they are part of attaining a fulfilled life. I am not sure if a person with a physical ailment could be fully happy and healthy, especially if the ailment could have been avoided in the first place, through having a healthier lifestyle.

Below are four aspects of taking care of physical health discussed:

- Healthy Diet
- Exercise
- Sleep Hygiene
- Body care

When one is ill, you feel weak and demotivated to follow your daily routine work. As a result it is very important to take care of the whole physical body in order to be healthy, happier and successful.

WHAT IS A GOOD DIETING?

A few years ago, a friend whom I will call Kate was always in the gym before and after work. She also had several diet plans that I did not agree with, but the more I tried to intervene, the more she resented me, so I decided to mind my own business. Nevertheless, Kate's body looked alright to most people, but she had lots of weight loss. I could hear some people really admire her especially other girls who wanted to be size zero like her or like the girls in the commercials and the films. Even so, there was some resistance from our health care professional friends, who, like me, felt that Kate's lifestyle was not healthy. But maybe our career background and experiences influenced our insight. Kate could eat oats in the morning, never drank milk but bought some protein powder which had been recommended by her gym instructor.

At some point she bought quite expensive ready-made meals online, which were shipped to her including some powdered stuff which she mixed with water. When I asked her the components of some of the stuff, she had no idea but believed it would help her remain in shape. Most times, what Kate ate was one good meal a day and snacked a few times a day on several seeds and that was it. Even so, Kate complained a lot of feeling tired all the time, her mood was always low and I noticed most times she looked like she had cried the whole night. But I decided to stick to my decision, to mind my own business even though I believed she was unhealthy and I could see traits of eating disorder. However, one day a very concerned friend suggested we check Kate's BMI (body mass index) and BP (body pressure) due to her constant fatigue. To our revelation Kate was below the healthy level and needed to pay attention on it. But was I surprised? No, I wasn't because I had watched her follow poor diet plans just because they were recommended to her and would help her lose weight.

I have seen a lot of young people like Kate, falling prey to wrong diet regimes which sometimes affect their bodies' immune system, energy levels, memory and concentration negatively. Even so every New Year, some people take on new healthy diet regimes and goals. Personally, I have been a culprit of taking on the challenge, only to give up a few weeks later. I am sure you did it too once or twice and you may know several people who did the same.

What is healthy dieting? Is it just done at a particular time of the year when you need to lose weight or should it be a lifestyle that is done with good insight and care?

There are several healthy diet books at our disposal and several advice commercials but I find them lacking the real information. I studied diploma in food technology which entailed food nutrition, food biology, food chemistry among other subjects. Prior to that, I had an insight into healthy eating in my school years when we partook a subject called 'home science', which included healthy eating as a core area of study. I have also helped people uptake healthy lifestyles including diet during my work.

Hence, I have insightful knowledge on diet but I still find a lot of people following diet plans that are not healthy, which are detrimental to their bodies and mental health. Hence I will discuss healthy eating at length. When, I worked with patients with eating disorders, I found it extremely despondent to see how detrimental poor diet (whether excessive or low) can do to one's body. Also to the person's mental health including memory, concentration and self-esteem.

Still, vitamins based foods and other nutrients can boost good mental health including memory, concentration and mood. Some ladies become addicted to dieting and they are unable to stop even when they reach the healthy level. Therefore it is crucial for one to eat healthy meals regularly at least 3 times a day and drink water regularly. One needs to make sure all the vital nutrients are available in all the meals including vitamins, proteins, carbohydrates and minerals and salts at right amount. One can check online on Health care websites like NHS Website from medical and health care professionals on the right amount of nutrients one needs. Also tell your doctor if you are worried you are overdoing your dieting.

Below is a simple chart showing you how to eat well;

EAT WELL

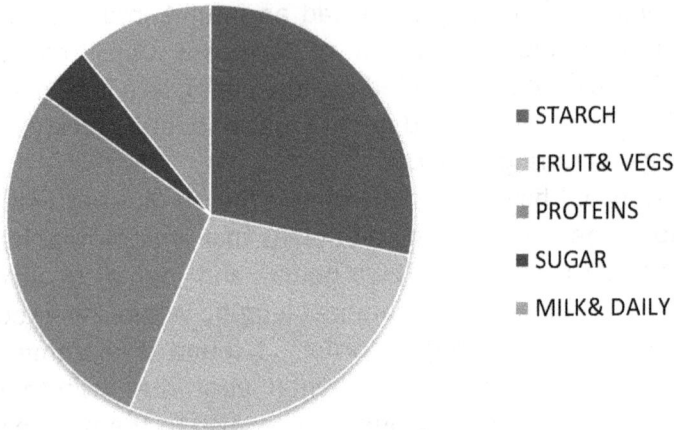

- STARCH
- FRUIT& VEGS
- PROTEINS
- SUGAR
- MILK& DAILY

Guidelines for a Healthy Diet

1. Enjoy your food. Do not perceive eating as a task, take your time to eat comfortably and slowly for good digestion and enjoyment of your meal. Eating food is a way of healthy living so enjoy it.
2. Eat a variety of different foods ie proteins, starch, vitamins and minerals.
3. Eat the right amount to be a healthy weight. You can check the details on NHS Website.
4. Eat plenty of foods rich in starch and fibre ie cereals, potatoes, whole grain, wholemeal bread
5. Eat plenty of fruits and vegetables (5-a-day) like oranges, kiwi, mangoes, passion, cabbage, beetroot, and spinach among others.
6. Don't eat too many foods that contain a lot of saturated fats like cheese and dairy products.
7. Don't have sugary foods and drinks. Have them as treats ie fizzy drinks, sweets, juices and cakes.
8. Drink lots of water at least 6 glasses a day.
   Women are the main buyers of foods among most

cultures and they are a great target of foods marketing and diet related advertising. Nonetheless, we all need to be vigilant of how we purchase, prepare and eat our foods, maintaining a healthy diet at all times with the correct calorie intake. Eating is of social and psychological as well as physiological importance, and eating thus contributes to our well-being and healthy living. As noted earlier in the chapter healthy eating helps your body's immune system, helps your memory, sleeping patterns, reduces anxiety and stress disorders and further improves your reproductive system, assists chemical balances in the body, among others.

Sicknesses related to poor diet:-
Scurvy, rickets, Marasmus, kwashiorkor, mineral deficiency- I combined these diseases, since most of the information is available in all healthcare facilities. Poor intake of diet without the right nutrients can lead to these deficiencies. One should be mindful of lack of enough minerals and vitamins in most foods. However, one gets the nutrients from eating a lot of fresh fruits and vegetables. Most of these nutrients can also be obtained through food supplements i.e. vitamins & minerals like Vitamin C, calcium, magnesium, zinc among others. It is always advisable to eat fresh fruits and vegetables daily and also whole meal, seeds, nuts, dairy products and fishy food.

Most of these diseases affect people in marginalised areas. Nonetheless, lack of supplements and sunlight can cause Rickets problems especially in countries with long winters leading to lack of Vitamin D. Pregnant women and children should be very mindful of eating the right foods since they highly need the nutrients.

Eating disorders- When one starts to eat less or more than needed by the body there are drastic changes to the body like changes to body weight, breathing problems, loss of energy levels among others. If one over eats they can suffer from **Obesit**y and they have excess weight gain and can struggle with healthy issues like breathing. One should avoid oil and sugary food and also junk food which are easily accessible in our society today.

On the other hand, for those who lose weight due to poor diet and fear of gaining weight they can suffer from **Anorexia Nervosa**. Most of these eating habits are influenced by poor mental states, where one is overly stressed and not conscious or not in control of their actions. If there is loss of control to poor eating habits, one should see a doctor.

Cardiovascular disease, hypertension, diabetes mellitus- These chronic diseases are related to diet intake where one's breathing and blood sugar is affected by their diet intake. Most people with obesity suffer from these disease but other diet problems can also cause the ailments. Hence, it is important to keep up with a good diet intake.

Osteoporosis- is a condition of the bones becoming weak. Eating problem? is not the main cause of the problem, however when one's diet is poor and not well balanced, the malnutrition can lead to the ailment. Young people whose bones are still forming should be aware of the danger of excessive dieting which can result in this problem.

Cancer- Most causes of cancer is due to our lifestyles which include what we put into our bodies, which includes foods, cigarette smoking and drinking alcohol. Eating a lot of red meats, high intake of sugar and increased usage of salts can raise the risk of cancer like bowel and stomach cancer respectively. Whilst eating foods high in fibre and having dairy products can reduce the risk of these cancers. Additionally, it is important to be aware of food we eat, since diet and obesity have been rated as causal factors of cancer. More so, for cancer patients and all other patients, it is advisable to maintain a healthy diet to boost the immune system. Most processed foods often have different ingredients that are not helpful to our body, which is why it is important to eat organic and fresh healthy food.

BENEFITS OF REGULAR EXERCISE

They said too much work without play makes Jack a dull boy. I think Jack would also be unhealthy and stressed. Exercise should be on your weekly routine, if not daily. Good exercise helps you to reduce stress, since you are able to switch off our minds from daily activities. Indeed it has been reported that **good exercise reduces depression and other health problems** including the one I mentioned earlier of cardiovascular problems and obesity.

Indeed, physical exercise enhances our fitness, so we are flexible and more energetic in our daily life. The stress hormones in our body are also broken hence the rate of being overwhelmed by issues becomes less. Outdoors, activities like football, going for a run also helps us get out of congested and stressful environment helping to clear our minds. The fresh air is helpful to our breathing systems and our mind's creativity is also enhanced.

If you are like me, exercise is like marmite. Some people like it, others like me do not. Still, it is a necessary evil, if we need to live longer and healthier lives. I try my best every week to join a zumba class for my weekly exercise. But to be honest, every week I always find a good excuse to give to my husband so that he can let me off from attending my class. Nevertheless, my husband never gives in to my made up excuses unless they are really genuine. Yet, after every class I always come home and thank him for pushing me to the class, since I feel happier, energetic and accomplished.

I would encourage you, if you are like me and you need pushing to the gym, seek support from other people. Try to make a habit to join an exercise regime that you enjoy and that you can follow and appoint watchmen to support you. You need regular exercise for your health and productivity.

How to get support for exercise;
- Join a gym and ask for personal trainer support to keep you going
- Join an exercise group with friends or acquaintances, so that you can do it together ie evening walk or run, cycling or swimming sessions, aerobics, football or tennis club
- Join a dance class or swimming lessons which will help you exercise
- Put reminders for exercise times in your diary or in your phone

- Buy exercise equipment which you can use at home as you watch TV or baby sit ie skipping rope, exercise DVD 's or exercise indoor on a bike, or on a mat.
- Have a reward plan i.e. if you exercise every week then treat yourself
- Have a fixed exercise aim or goal i.e. what do you want to achieve from the exercise ie shape your thighs, loose tummy weight etc.
- Review your exercise regime regularly

Advantages of Good exercise

Cardiovascular system- Heart rate is maintained, respiration and blood circulation is enhanced reducing risk of cardiac arrest, stroke and heart attacks.

Immune system- Strengthens our body muscles and body movements. Also the body metabolisms work better including digestion, absorption of nutrients, excretion, fluid regulation and also thermoregulation. Overall, when the body functions properly the immune system is high.

Depression- when one's body system works well, then feeling of tiredness and low mood are reduced. Exercise also helps with improving one's esteem since overweight issues and illnesses are reduced.

Sleep improvement- it has been reported that good exercise improves sleep patterns and reduces rates of insomnia.

Brain function- due to good blood flow and rest from good sleep which increases due to regular exercise, the brain creativity and functioning is enhanced. Also brain functions improvements include our learning and memory getting better. Moreover, reductions of the risk of having degenerative brain diseases like dementia.

Body weight- Obesity is linked to the risk of cancer for bowel and pancreatic cancer (Cancer research UK). Hence, exercise will help one maintain the correct body mass index reducing cancer risk among other diseases related to obesity.

Over-exercise can cause problems like cardiac arrest, stroke and muscle tear. One needs to work out to their capability and try not to overwork. You remember I mentioned my friend Kate who was on a poor diet and going to the gym twice a day. As I stated, her levels of energy were low and maybe I did not mention her immune system too was not very strong. At the same time she appeared to have depressive mood due to her poor diet and over exercise. Hence, it is commendable if we watch out how we exercise and the reasons why we do it. Is it to keep healthy and fit or is it to prove a point, or to compete with other people. We all have different body mass, height and shapes. Hence it would not be wise to try and be all size zero as many ladies try to do. Check your weight and maintain it between the health standards. The health tables can be found in government hospitals, on the internet and also in the gym. However be mindful of getting credible sources of information.

SLEEP HYGIENE

Sleep helps our brains to slow down and rest, which is very important for all human beings. It also allows the body to wear and tear. Statistics indicates that more than 10 million prescriptions of sleeping pills are given each year in England, which only offers a short-term relief (NHS 2012). It important to have good night sleeps for healthy life and productivity. Psychologists have referred to sleep as a behaviour, where our body rests but our mind consciousness is still awake, but not in the same way as when we are fully awake. That is why we have dreams once we are asleep which we sometimes remember.

Most adults require 6-8 hours sleep daily hence we spend 1/3 of our lives asleep for us to maintain good health. However, if we have sleep problems like **Insomnia** then it affects our functioning. Insomnia affects almost 25% of population (Carlson 2007). Most people try to correct insomnia through medication which is a quick fix but not a long term remedy. To be able to overcome insomnia, one need to maintain healthy lifestyle, as outlined later in the chapter. At the same time, it is important to know the cause of sleep problems which could be the condition of the bedroom; maybe too much light or being in a noisy area. Also, one could be taking medication which interferes with the sleeping patterns.

Our lifestyles too can impact to our sleeping problems. For example for the people who work at night and sleep during the day, their routine can cause be * disorganised. Other people can have sleep attacks, where they have urges to sleep during the day especially in the afternoon and then one finds it difficult to sleep at night. Other people snore while sleeping, hence they can interrupt their own sleep or the sleep of others in the same room or house.

Vivid dreams can also interrupt our sleep, especially if they are scary and sometime they are as a result of what we are exposed to during the day, for example scary movies or scary bed time stories. If there are difficult situations in our lives we can suffer from broken sleep patterns, for example if one has a health issue like being diagnosed with a terminal illness or they have a painful physical body part (like a broken leg or a twisted arm).

Other kinds of emotional distress like depression or stress issues like relationships, work issues or financial problems can affect our sleeping patterns and need to be addressed promptly.

There are other people who find it difficult to breathe while sleeping known as **sleep apnoea,** which can affect their sleeping patterns. **Sleep paralysis** is where people when asleep or trying to wake up briefly find it difficult to move. Overall, there are many sleeping disorders, hence if one notices a persisting pattern of sleep concerns despite trying regular sleep hygiene tips given in this book, then it would be advisable to see a doctor. Subsequently, our sleep patterns can hugely affect our health, productivity and also our life enjoyment when we are sleep deprived.

Maintaining Healthy Sleep;
- Good exercise routine regularly and getting outdoors for daylight
- Eating healthy and not too late.
- Avoiding sleep debts- not sleeping well for many days.

- Make the bedroom area pleasant- clean, quiet, well ventilated, dim light and comfortable bed.
- Make a time routine when to go to bed every day and stick to it.
- Drink something warm & soothing to help you sleep like hot chocolate, ovaltine etc.
- Watch calm TV programmes in the evenings & listen to relaxing music.
- Avoid taking stimulants before going to bed like coffee, smoking, alcohol, cola and chocolates.
- Avoid watching scary movies just before going to bed.
- Keep tv's, laptops, Ipads, books out of the bed room area.
- Have a soothing bath before sleep.
- If awake at night for more than 30 minutes get up and go to another room read/keep busy and go to bed when ready to sleep; helps your mind learn that bedroom is for sleeping only.
- Deal with day's issues, conflicts, worries before evening to avoid staying awake at night.
- Have an alarm clock to wake you up in the morning to stop you from worrying.
- Keep your mobile phone off or silent during the night for a good sleep.
- Try sleeping without using sleeping pills to avoid drug dependency insomnia.

OVER-ALL BODY CARE

Good hygiene is about cleaning our bodies, our environment and being aware of what we put into our bodies. We were taught this at a young age. However, I will just mention in brief tips of body care for a quick reminder, otherwise I will not have addressed the whole issue of health. Some of the diseases in our society are also due to poor body care. These include **gum diseases, toe nails problems and skins diseases like dandruff, scabies and ringworms**. Sometimes, we have the information and try to do it regularly, but we are not consistent enough, especially with our attention to our environmental health sometimes and also our diet intake and the products we let into our bodies. Moreover, it is vital to go for regular medical check-ups for example for dental check-up and for women regular cervical tests, mammogram among others.

The **body care products** we use can sometimes end up affecting our bodies negatively. Hence, it is imperative for us to try and use medically proven products on our skin, hair and body. Anything that comes in contact with your skin you should be very vigilant. Some people are allergic to some chemical used in these products, and sometime the effect can be tragic. The beauty products used by most women can have negative effect to their body in the future hence it is important to be aware of what you expose yourself to. In our world today we see high rate of women with esteem issues, always trying to look like somebody else or trying to appear differently. I am not against looking beautiful. You do the best you can, however it is paramount that you do not risk your own health in the process.

I saw a lady on the TV media who had used a beauty product to enhance her beauty and unfortunately it reacted critically; she lost her limbs (both legs and arms). She was very regretful of her mistakes. Some people might not have similar effect, but at times I wonder why the rate of cancer is so high on women. Apart from our environment and diet, it is important to beware that the products we put into our bodies are not harmful. **Some people take tablets to lose weight or to change their skin complexion.** If they are dark they want to be lighter, if they are light they want to be darker. Others opt for cosmetic plastic surgery which at times comes with baggage of health scares, financial implications among others. From my psychology studies, your feelings of how you look and your confidence are mostly shaped by your self-esteem. Hence, it would be helpful if you deal with your self-esteem issues instead of trying to change the outer you, mould the inner self.

Addiction to prescription drugs is also another concern related to taking care of our bodies. Some people are addicted to legal prescription drugs and also to non-prescription legal drugs. However, some of the issues we are trying to overcome, we can do it.

Most people in Britain are reported to be addicted to pain relief tablets which help them cope with constants headaches resulting from stressful lifestyles, sleep problems and poor diet and lack of exercise. If most of these people were committed to deal with the issues causing stress in their lives by at least adopting healthier lifestyle, then they won't need the painkillers. Indeed, they get used to the pills until they get immune and hence they keep increasing the dosage. The effect of living on painkillers can be detrimental to body functions but also to mental health. Unfortunately we have seen celebrities who were addicted to prescribed drugs that lead them to their deathbeds. So beware of getting addicted to prescribed or non-prescribed drugs. Stop before it is too late.

Other people use **illegal drugs** to cope with issues. Most people start off as fun for recreation or as one off for coping. Nonetheless, they become addicted to an extent, it becomes irreversible. Other people take drugs to stay awake and concentrate on specific assignments and before they know it, they can't work without the drug. The drug use becomes detrimental to their bodies and also to their mental health. Indeed, use of drugs can trigger mental illnesses like depression and psychotic disorders. Brain function can also be impaired in the brain cortex region, leading to inappropriate behaviour. Taking illegal drugs is a crime and possession of these drugs can lead you to jail and you might lose more than you intended. It can also lead one to have unprotected sex which can lead to contracting sexually transmitted diseases like **HIV** or even have unwanted pregnancies among other issues.

Equally, I have seen some people who started off with a glass of wine a day and eventually became alcoholic. Excessive uses of **alcohol** have health problems like lung disease, kidney problems and cancer. There are social effects which include relationship problems, social issues and risk of losing all you have worked for. **Smoking** cigars, tobacco and cigarettes have harmful effect to health including cancer, teeth problems, lung problems among others.

Overall, good self-care will take you a long way. Do it healthily, actively and wisely.

Tips for overall body care:

- Shower at least once a day, use sun protection cream during sunny seasons.
- Brushing our teeth at least twice a day.
- Changing clothes every day.
- Changing our beddings weekly.
- Living in a clean environment like clean house, well lighted and ventilated.
- Clean and moisturise your hands regularly and care for your nails.
- Avoid contact with other people's bodily fluids. Always use protective gloves when touching bodily fluids and clean with alcohol and soap later.
- Have regular health check-ups like dentist, cervical tests for women etc.
- Avoid using untested body and skin care products that are not medically proven.
- Avoid taking drugs, and excessive alcohol, drinking and smoking.
- Avoid using prescription drugs where you can apply other healthy means to cope with life issues.
- Avoid surgical body changes unless for healthy reason like breast implants, lip enhancements etc.
- Take care when having sex. Avoid careless and unprotected sex.
- Seek medical attention when you have persistent body ailments and infections.

In conclusion to this topic on physical health, it is helpful to notice the importance of having a good physical health. What happens to your body and to your minds correlates, so take care of them. When your mind and body are healthy, then you can enjoy life more. Indeed, you have the strength to go out each day to follow your dreams. Most times we neglect our health only to feel low, frustrated and weak. Now that you have the tips, then keep practicing them and you will enjoy a long healthy and happier life.

CHAPTER 3:BUILDING RELATIONSHIPS

While I was busy chasing after my dreams, working long nights in a forensic hospital and studying for my degree during my days off, I didn't realise how my personality changed over the years. I had become impatient, irritable and hard to get along with. My behaviour was noticeable to my colleagues, friends and all those who came around me. Even the traffic lights were aware of my impatience that is why I got a speeding ticket. Eventually, the intensity of my behaviour was brought to light by a caring brave colleague who pointed out how I had been behaving at work, frequently getting into heated exchanges with colleagues. This revelation was very shocking as I reflected on my bad behaviour. From then henceforth, I decided to make amends and to work on my behaviour and attitude, learning to be more patient with others. The change didn't happen overnight, but through persistence. First, I went on a holiday to relax and I also read books on relationships. I also started to observe other people as they interacted and I often analysed my own performance. To my surprise, my bad temper was not just due to current stress but was also as a result of backlog of previous pains over the years. My negative attitudes and behaviour towards others had been distorted by accumulated unattended hurt feelings. Hence, change was inevitable and I will share some of the lessons I learnt.

Overall, in our daily life we interact with other people often. Wherever you go, you have to associate with other people based on regular interaction, solidarity, love or other social engagements. We can never avoid relationships with others when we are alive. Indeed, **humans are social beings and have an emotional need to socialise and interact with each other**. We all need to be loved and appreciated by those around us. However, our interactions can either be enjoyable and productive or painful and dysfunctional. Therefore, we all need to have appropriate social skills to build healthy relationships. Indeed, in relationships people tend to influence each other and become interdependent as they share thoughts, feelings, activities and intimacy. Consequently, our close relationships can affect our health, our mannerisms and also our motivation to achieve in life, hence we need to cultivate decent relationships. This should be done in our families, our schools, our neighbourhoods, at work and with people in our nations and across the world.

When relationships grow, there is an emotional attachment, which can be either secure or insecure. In healthy relationships there is security and trust, whilst in dysfunctional relationships there is insecurity and a lot of emotional pain. Nevertheless, **communication is the core ingredient to building good relationships**. Certainly, how we communiqué across with each other through respect and clarity is vital. Poor communication can cause misunderstanding and conflicts. Other factors like personality and cultural differences and dissimilar perspectives can affect how we relate to each other. Moreover, relationships also change over time, hence it is important for one to be aware of their surroundings and ideologies adjoining different aspects of relationships and how we relate in different settings. Still, one has to be mindful of the environment he/she chooses to expose to and how the relationships shape the individual's life. **Being aware of the associates you choose is vital for they will influence you** in many ways including your actions, ideologies, choices and behaviour.

DYSFUCTIONAL RELATIONSHIPS

These are relationships where parties in the relationships are neither respected nor emotionally supported. In these relationships there is emotional turmoil and poor communication is fostered. There is also co-dependency where one feels hopelessly entangled with the other person. The relationship is toxic and one suffers. These types of relationships are seen in our daily lives and it is important to identify them.

Most dysfunctional families where there is physical and verbal aggression exhibit this type of relationships.

Other examples of relationships are in peers' relationships where one is bullied and disrespected and made to live in fear. Bullying is very evident among young people and also sometimes among adults peers. One's self esteem is affected negatively in these types of relationships. People who work under pressure and feel they do not have a right to address their concerns also have this type of relationship with their colleagues or with their bosses. No one should live feeling inferior and traumatised in any relationship. Studies also confirm that, children who are brought-up in disorganised and insecure relationships by their care givers grow up with distorted perceptions of what good relationships entails. Most of these individuals have negative core-beliefs that they are not lovable and they do not deserve respect. As a result, when they are abused they just accept it. Some psychology studies indicate that some children from domestic abusive homes grow up to be abusers or marry abusive partners, while other become prostitutes and are subjected to abuse. Nevertheless, not all children from abusive homes end up in abusive relationships, but the highest percentage do. Hence, it is vital to identify signs of dysfunctional relationships and address the situations early.

The Europe council (2002) reported that 1 in 4 women face domestic violence in their life time. More studies by the Department of health UK (2002) have shown that almost ¾ of a million children each year in UK witness domestic violence. Home office UK (2004) has reported that 16% of domestic abuse reported half of it is due to violence. Some police reports have revealed that in UK every minute there is a report of domestic violence. BBC News (Nov 2013) also reported that two women are killed every week as a result of domestic cruelty. It is crucial to be aware of what entails in dysfunctional relationships that end up in abuse, violence and sometimes murder of the parties involved. These kinds of violence are as a result of dysfunctional relationships and are not just in UK but all over the world. UK statistics are well gathered than most of other countries, but I know there are many other countries where abuse Is even worse but rarely talked about due to ignorance, fear and cultural oppression.

However, nobody should live in these kinds of circumstances.
SIGNS OF DSYFUCTIONAL RELATIONSHIPS:

- Verbal and physical aggression and violence
- Inferiority or superiority complex.
- Manipulation and controlling behaviour.
- Poor or lack of communication.
- Feelings of fear, guilt, insecurity, social isolation and dependency.
- Emotional turmoil, jealousy, obsession, resentment.
- Imbalance of power and feeling trapped.
- Tension in the relationship and loneliness.
- Anxiety and depression.

Once you identify some of these signs of dysfunctions in your relationships like I did when my colleague pointed out my behaviour as mentioned earlier in the chapter it is important to address the issues promptly through good communication with the parties involved. You need to have good communications skills and to remain assertive. For example if a friend has been disrespectful to you clearly outline your concern, trying not to blame the other person, but tell them how their behaviour makes you feel. Then, wait for their response and then agree on a way forward. Make sure the issue is addressed and there is point of action. It is also important to have a follow up plan and a review date. If there is positive change then keep up with the plan. Most relationships deteriorate because parties concerned do not communicate their feelings and when they do, they do not strategically point out their plan or review progress.

Laying boundaries in relationships helps to overcome overbearing and abuse behaviour. One has to remain assertive in relationships. For example, at work you need to know the work guidelines and to be mindful of your responsibilities. Every so often, if a boss keeps overworking you with obligations that are not part of your role, then you need address these issues and draw the boundaries professionally and effectively. Sometimes even well-meaning friends can abuse your time and resources. Hence, **it is important to**

have boundaries and to remain assertive. If someone really cares for you and is ethical then, they should be respectful of your needs. At the same time, it is equally important for you to respect other people's principles and boundaries. Where there is disrespect and poor communication, the relationship becomes dysfunctional displaying signs above. But there are ways to resolve issues and conflicts in relationships.

CONFLICT RESOLUTION TIPS IN RELATIONSHIPS:
- Raise the issues with the other person on a neutral ground.
- Describe the issues and how they make you feel without blaming the other person.
- Request action and co-operation from the other party.
- Agree on the action plan.
- Follow through with the plan.
- Review the plan after a set time.

If the problems persist, it would be better **to seek intervention through supportive and mature individuals who are in a position to assist.** The authorities can also help in cases of abuse especially domestic abuse, physical and sexual abuse. In our world today we are daily captivated by the rate of children being murdered after long time of abuse, without anyone blowing the whistle. Also there is high rate of domestic abuse and work related victimization and also bullying in schools. It is our individual responsibility to help victims of abuse or to alert authorities when we realise somebody is being subjected to torture.

Sometimes, most people in abusive relationships feel helpless and they are afraid of the abuser, hence they find it difficult to talk. However, there are many agencies of government and charities that help people in these kinds of circumstances. Ultimately, if relationship problems are not resolved and parties involved are still not respected and supported, it is significant to terminate the relationship before it affect your physical and mental health and sometimes even your other areas of life including your career and your finances.

Do not let recurring conflicts and dysfunctional behaviour in relationships go unresolved, be pro-active to address them effectively.

HEALTHY RELATIONSHIPS

For successful, healthy and happy living, one needs to cultivate decent and healthy relationships. We all should aim at building healthy relationships which are hard work but worth having. First you have to evaluate the kinds of present relationships you have with other people and articulate how far you want the relationships to go. Then lay boundaries that guide the relationships honouring both parties' needs and principles.

At the same time, it is important to know that our personalities, circumstances and perceptions can affect our role in the relationships. Hence, initially deal with any negativity in your life that might be projected into your relationships, for example prejudices on various social aspects, or past negative experiences that might be transferred to how you relate with certain people.

Over the years I have learnt that there are three categories of people you will come across in life; which are acquaintances, associates and confidants. It is very easy to confuse these categories and this mistake might lead to hurt due to unfulfilled expectations. Therefore, how you identify these individuals and relate to them will help you have decent relationships. Moreover, you will evade unrealistic expectations from relationships with wrong groups of people. **Impractical anticipations in relationships can lead to unmet needs and can eventually lead to hurt feelings and pain of broken hearts.** Hence, it is imperative to know what category of friendship or relationships you have and what role these people play in your life.

Acquaintances-These are people you have met in settings of your career or social interests. You do not know them well but you have shared selected engagements with them. Do not confuse them as your true friends, for their interest is in the activity you have shared but not you. They can also be part of social activities you engage from time to time, like fighting against injustice or poverty or greenbelt movement or part of your gym or book club etc.

Associates- These are people who you have come to know very well and you have engaged with severally. They might be interested in the same kind of areas you are interested like in career or work in the same organisation or live in the same neighbourhood. They can also be part of a religious or political sector which you belong to. You will interact with these people often and they act like close friends, since they end up knowing you well and being **companions** in various areas and seasons of your life. Conversely, they are not lifetime friends and if the cause changes they move on. Sometimes we expect these people to be our lifetime friends hence when they leave we can get very hurt, since we had become acquitted with them. However, their role in your life is seasonal so, you should expect change and learn to accept it.

Confidants- They are the life time friends who are with you through thick and thin. They know your real self in bad and good times. They do not judge you and they do not care about your failures, they love you anyway. Confidants are very few to come across. I have realised most confidants are either family members or people you met when you were young. They get into your business and they tell you off when you are wrong. They also assist you when your life gets messy and they are honestly happy for you when you succeed. You feel free with them because you do not have to put on a persona to be around them. They are in your **inner circle of friends** and they bring the best out of you, help you in your dreams and believe in you and love you unconditionally. These are the people you should share your dreams and secretes with.

Additionally, to knowing the type of relationships you have, it is important to be secure in ourselves to form healthy relationships. An individual needs to have a good self-esteem and to be self-confidence. One needs not to put their ego and self-value on the relation but need to have inner emotional stability. One also needs to be aware of their role and to accept the role but also be aware that the role can change.

Most people coming from healthy family background with less traumatic experiences in life are secure and are most likely to have healthy relationships. Even so, people who have undergone traumatic life setbacks like divorces, illnesses, loss or abusive relationships can overcome the trauma with time and through support, and they can still build good relationships. Hence as pointed out, self-awareness is crucial to forming healthy relationships. Nonetheless, other key needs to healthy relationships are commitment, boundaries and respect.

CHARACTERISTICS OF HEALTHY RELATIONSHIPS:

* All parties feel respected and honoured.
* There is trust, integrity, understanding and equality.
* Effective communication, commitment and co-operation.
* Self-awareness, boundaries and accountability.
* Empathy, compassion, support and nurturing.
* Capitalises on positives and helps each other on set goals.
* Inter-dependency rather than co-dependency.
* Spending quality time, fun, joy and contentment
* Each party takes responsibility.
* There is **NO** form of any abuse - no emotional, verbal or physical abuse.
* Recreation time and relaxation.
* Feelings of self-worth and emotional stability.

PERSONALITIES IN RELATIONSHIPS

So do you classify yourself as an Introvert or an extrovert? Are you Sanguine, Phlegmatic, Choleric or Melancholy? Most of our conflicts and misunderstandings can be due to personality clash. If we knew our strengths and weaknesses and further acknowledged other peoples' strengths and flaws, our relationships at work, at home and in our marriages would be better. There would be less conflicts, feuds, jealousy and anger. Overall, understanding our personality and the personalities of people we interact with on day to day life would reduce the high rate of conflicts, stress and anxiety disorders. Indeed, we would overcome a lot of divorces, suicide rates and depression when we are getting along with others at home and at work improving our life satisfaction, health, success and productivity.

Here are some strong and weak traits for different personalities;

Sanguine: *Strengths-* outgoing, enjoys happy emotions, talkative, leads, artistic, optimistic, extrovert and fun to be with.

Weaknesses- undisciplined, forgetful, not good in comforting others, likes attention and loud.

Choleric: *Strengths-* leader, decisive, strong willed, unemotional, competitive, confident, controls, organised, outspoken, optimistic, extrovert.

Weakness- impatient can be rude, bossy and unsympathetic.

Melancholy: *Strengths-* analytic, emotional, artistic, soft-spoke, pessimistic, introvert, orderly and self-sacrificial.

Weakness- get hurts or depressed easily, perfectionist, unpopular, moody and withdrawn.

Phlegmatic: *Strengths-* analytic, pessimistic, introvert, easy going, adaptable, patient, submissive and balanced.

Weakness- shy, don't like conflicts, can tend to be lazy, blank, fearful, worrier, indecisive.

Most people have more than one personality trait, but among the traits there are 1 or 2 most dominant personalities. Most of us marry spouses with opposite personalities, because we admire the differences. But as married couples we clash, if the differences are not well understood. Sanguine can marry melancholy while choleric can marry phlegmatic, then guess what happens if the differences are not appreciated? Yet, all personalities have weaknesses that can be worked on to have better relationships if the individuals are willing. However, we all need to understand each other and allow time and space to learn, without pointing out the flaws every day since we all have our personality weaknesses. Then our relationships will get better and our lives become more productive and happier.

EXITING ENDED RELATIONSHIPS

An acquaintance I will call Rose met a young handsome man called Jack in a friend's birthday party. They exchanged phone numbers and a week later Rose and Jack met for a first date. A few months down the line they were heads over heels in love and were inseparable. Everyone admired their relationship and before long they had moved in to live together. After several months, Rose informed us that they were having problems and their relationship was very toxic. She appeared very distressed and frightened to go back to home. The friends counselled her and took her back to her house and they further tried to intervene, by talking to both of them on how to resolve issues. These good friends also informed Rose she could go to their houses if she wanted to leave Jack, but she declined the offer. They additionally gave Rose the information that she needed for emergency and support for domestic violence helplines. Rose appeared fine for a while and reported to the friends that they had made up with Jack. Nonetheless, three months later she came back to friends crying that she had been kicked out by Jack from the house and he was seeing another lady. By this time Rose was two months pregnant, jobless and homeless.

The friends were very understanding and helpful to Rose and within six months she was back on her feet. She found a job that she could work from home and had a house and was now ready to be a single mother. Then, Jack tried to come back to her life when she had stabilised but by this time Rose had known the magic of closing the doors and exiting completely. Nevertheless, I wish she had done it earlier before she lost her first job and got herself pregnant. Even so, now Rose is a happy mother of a bouncing baby girl, she is stable and Jack has supervised visitation to see his daughter. At some point Rose had to exit for her boyfriend's dysfunctional relationship in order to live a healthy and productive life.

Overall, I do not blame those who choose to discontinue toxic dysfunctional relationships and marriages through separation or divorce, subsequently having experienced emotional and physical abuse. I suggest they have support and counselling to rebuild back their lives again. Nonetheless, I advocate for resolving issues that face marriages and doing our best to make relationships work. But if you have done what it takes and nothing changes, then it is wiser to move on to avoid more hurt to you and to those close to you.

Indeed, some relationships in our lives have to end and we need to exit prudently. When relationship doors close in our lives like in love, marriage, work, business, neighbours, friends and family, we need to gather strength and do it promptly and effectively to reduce hurt feelings and wasting time crying on dead horses. Doors can close as a result of conflicts, transfer, death, divorce, misunderstanding, abuse or even change of values and goals. Some closures are unexpected and others are not anticipated. The art of closing these doors is important so as to be able to deal with the loss, then to overcome grief, emptiness and try to move on.

I have met people in my social life circles and also in my work life that are aware that some doors are closed, but they are unwilling to accept it. Their denial has led to a lot of pain and time wasting, that they regretted in the end. Indeed, some people end up being emotionally and physically abused by people they would have let go many years before. Then, as the person drags their feet to accept the reality, they lose more than they needed to.

It is very important to close doors that are not helpful to our lives. Stop fighting to keep constituents and comrades around when their assignment ends in your life, please kiss them good bye. Moreover, if relationships are very toxic and you have tried to resolve the issues with no effect, I advise you to exit the door promptly. That includes friendships, jobs, acquaintances or associations that are detrimental to your health, happiness and progress. When these doors close, do not get bitter but choose to get better by forgiving and letting go. Choose to focus on the productive and positive areas of your life.

Tips for exiting closed doors:
- In overdue positions or abusive relationships close the doors at the right time; don't do it out of emotions nor

procrastinate. Plan your exit and just do it! It is your call.

- When someone walks out of your life, let them go. You may miss them, but remember you weren't the one that gave up but you can't force them to stay.
- Accept the grieving period or hurt emotions. Have a cry over them or talk to an understanding friend.
- Close the relationship with gentleness, respect and integrity.
- Close the doors with kindness and forgiveness for others involved and for your own mistakes.
- Close the doors and make sure you fulfil your promises.
- Close the doors with courage, remain assertive and expectant of a better future.
- Allow time to heal after closing doors. Do not push yourself to move on too fast.
- Count your blessings. There are other positive things in your life like supportive people & past achievements.
- If terminated doors affect your wellbeing promptly seek help, whether medical or spiritual or counselling help or legal help.
- Take care of yourself physically, emotionally, spiritually and psychologically.
- Once you have moved on, try not to dwell on exited door. Like talking or thinking about the closed doors. Try to celebrate the opportunities ahead and lessons learned and move on completely.
- Focus on your life and follow your dreams.

CHAPTER 4. REACHING SUCCESS
IDENTIFYING YOUR PURPOSE AND DREAMS

A dream is an imagined idea where one pictures the future. A dream can appear sweet, yet extreme when shared with other people, it can look like fantasy. Nonetheless, most people's dreams have come true. Hence, even your dreams can come true if you follow them diligently and tirelessly. Indeed, if others have done it before you, then you can even do it better. As long as the dream is genuine, then it is achievable. Nevertheless, a true dream is not just an imagination, but should bring a sense of purpose in life. The passion can originate from our hearts as we grow up, and other times can be instigated in our adulthood through life experiences and self-awareness. These passions can sometimes look vague and confusing, but over time they are unfolded as we go through life. Your purpose is aligned with what you feel passionate about in life. You must adore your dreams for you to be able to follow them through because they do not come easy. Examples of dreams are like mentoring young people, or eradicating poverty, supporting the old, or educating others, or inventing a car, or getting a medical cure for a specific ailment, or following a specific course of justice, or religion, or career.

One of the most famous dreams of our times is by **Dr Martin Luther King Junior,** an African- American Clergyman and a leader for civil rights movement. When campaigning against racial segregation, he stated that *'I have a dream that my four little children will one day live in a nation where they will not be judged by the colour of their skin, but by the content of their character.'*

His dream was a great passion and a sense of purpose. Dr Martin Luther King did his best to contest for what he believed and even lost his life for it. Although he did not live to see it come true, his dream and legacy has lived for many decades. Moreover, his children lived the dream of their father, where colour is less adjudicated.

From King's dream we can identify several steps he partook to reach it. First, he identified his dream, second he made a strategic plan to achieve it, thirdly he shared his dream with other people who helped campaign for it and also support him financially. Additionally he worked tirelessly to see the dream come true. Throughout his work he maintained a respectable character while advocating for peace, justice and respect among all people. So now we have explored on Dr King's dream, I would like you to reflect honestly on these questions about your life.

1. **What are the dreams in your life?**
2. **What is the purpose for your life?**
3. **Do you have a strategic plan to reach your dreams and have you achieved them yet?**

I suggest you take some time to reflect on these questions because they will save you a lot of years of regret. They can also shape your future steps and choices. Just like Dr Martin Luther King, think more how you are going to reach these dreams and make strategic plans. Dreaming is not good enough, but planning and going after your dreams is imperative. Moreover, the processes of dream achievements are crucial to acquiring a fulfilled life. Even so, sometimes we can follow other peoples' dreams and other times we can just go through life without dreams. Supplementary* we can have dreams and talk about them and never follow through. The true meaning of life is following your dreams and seeing most of them come to pass. You do not need to live a life by just going to work and going home without a purpose or passion. Most people work in jobs they are not passionate about and they spend most of their lives complaining and mourning, whilst they could have spent one afternoon reviewing their life purpose, dreams and passions. Some other people have followed their family or friends' dreams and forgotten their own dreams.

I urge you take time and ask yourself; first - **where are you in life?** Secondly - **Are you following your dreams?**

If the answer is **NO**, then reconsider and change your course.

A dream is derived by passion, purpose and ability, nevertheless a dream needs to be clearly defined so as to be consummated. When we define what we want to accomplish, then we portrait a **VISION**. A 'Vision' is when the dream is made clearer through planning and laying strategies. Thus, you need to identify the aims and objectives of achieving your vision.

A Vision should be clear and concise so that you can sensibly and effectively follow it through. Then one day the dream can come true.

A great visionary who inspired me as a teenager is the great American neurosurgeon Dr. Ben Carson, the author of the book '**Think Big**'. As a young boy growing up in the inner-city of Detroit, Ben was surrounded by poverty and saw a lot of people suffer with no means for good health care. As a result, he decided that when he grew up he would to do something about it. His life purpose was defined by his dream and passion to make a difference against poverty. He had a vision to become a doctor. As a result, he worked hard at school against all odds, till he became one of the re-known neurosurgeon and an author of many books. Dr Ben Carson has been involved in great works around the world and his work was even honoured by the American ex-president George Bush. Consequently, his dream to make a difference came true and has also inspired many people.

I must admit his book shaped my life significantly as a teenager girl growing up in Africa. Recollecting, Dr Ben Carson did not come from a glamorous background, but he had a dream and the resilience to see his vision accomplished.

Each of us has the ability to follow and accomplish the dreams in our hearts despite our circumstances. Our dreams should be bigger than us. If your dream is all about you, then it is not big enough. Dream about making a difference and solving problems for others in which ever arena you might be passionate about.

DREAM BIG- A big dream is exciting and gives us meaning to life and also challenges us to move outside our comfort zones and when we have finally accomplished the dream the sense of purpose is great. More so, if the purpose is to help other people, then more people will gain from us accomplishing our dreams and visions.

Nonetheless, not all of us are meant to be founders of organisations or to work in charitable organisation or to help others directly. But whatever you do, you can solve problems for others. A good scenario is how Bill Gates revolutionised the computer world which influenced computer programming all over the world. I believe Bill Gates and his associates could have been in their offices trying to solve a problem that was bigger than them, which eventually helped millions of people and also solved their own problems. Their persistence led to accomplishing their goal and becoming world changers. Same to you, you can become world changer for your life, your family your society or your nation if you persistently follow and accomplish your dreams.

Questions that will help you identify and reach your dreams:

What are your **dreams in life**? What are you **passionate** about? (Wealth, freedom, justice, success, character, peace, family, relationships, faith, independence, education...)

What are your **strengths** and values? What are your limitations?

What is the **Vision** towards reaching your dreams? What are your aims and Objectives?

What **steps** are you taking daily towards reaching your Vision or Goal post?

Who can support you to reach your life Goals?

How often are you **reviewing your goals progress**?

To identify our dreams, vision and goals, we need **self-awareness** and **creativity**. Being aware of our ability, talents and passions helps us make life choices that are attractive and of interest to us. Hence, career or life paths should be chosen in the way of our interest to maintain motivation, resilience and enjoyment in whatever dream we choose to follow. Additionally, our creativity whilst accomplishing dreams, determines our difference which paves our way up. When you know your difference, then you create **opportunities** to breakthrough mediocrity. I believe most of us want to go above average but we fear to be different. However,

our difference determines the height our talent, ability and creativity will get us to. Hence as you plan your dream and solve problems, maximise on your talent and uniqueness to shape your vision. Indeed when you look around the advertisements industry, the uniqueness of the product determines its' success in the market. The same in our life too, if you want to succeed then you have to be creative and take opportunities available. Every opportunity is important, especially if you are starting from ground zero, never despise small beginnings for they will usher you to greater heights.

Overall, when our goals, visions and life purpose are accomplished, then we become **successful**. Still, success needs to be balanced in all areas of our life including our health, relationships, social life and also our goals and life dreams. It is not worth it to accomplish a life dream in your career and then lose your health or lose your marriage. Hence it is vital to strike the balance. At the same time, you have to know that being successful doesn't necessarily make you great. What makes you great is when you are able to reach back and help somebody else become great. So help others in your world to accomplish their dreams too.

Beware of Success Nemeses:

Fear, Doubt, Indifference, Over-caution, Procrastination, Laziness, Stress, Pride, Naysayers, Mediocrity, Lack of integrity, Deception, Ignorance, Negative mind-sets, Poor planning, Poor health, Destructive habits, Negative associations and distractions.

SMART GOALS PLANNING

Without a vision, life appears to have no purpose. Some studies have indicated that people with goals live longer than people without goals in life. Still, a vision without strategic goals planning can be impractical. Hence, one needs to identify their goals and plan them well, through considering SMART STEPS to follow. Likewise as you plan to follow your goals, it is important to know that you have to sacrifice to get what you want. You also need to identify things in your life that are of no importance and be willing to let them go, so that you can accomplish your goals. Moreover, as you identify goals, it is important to know that they can take time and you will face challenges, but be willing to keep up the fight. You have to be assertive for your goals and cut off distractions. Constantly too, you have to motivate yourself most of the times. You also have to make a commitment to do something every day towards your goal. The process can be daunting but it is valuable and in the end it's all worth it. There will be a sense of life accomplishment, so keep going, do not give up.

Setting Smart Goals:

Once you have identified your aims and objectives for your vision. Then you need **smart steps** to make your goal workable. **SMART-** SPECIFIC, MEASURABLE, ATTAINABLE, REALISTIC AND TIME BOUND.

Specific- be detailed and clear about your goals. Outlining what you want to achieve and by when. This should be well defined to avoid confusion and derailing from the vision. *Is it a career, relationship, health, losing weight? What are you aiming to attain and by when?*

Measurable- make your goals steps in a way you can be able to measure with time. You need to monitor your goals consistently, and as you monitor you need a measurement for example time measurement, exams measurement or financial gain or growths in knowledge or vision that will help you measure if you are progressive, stagnant or regressing.

Attainable – your goal should be something you can achieve or attain. You should have the ability, the time and the means to follow the steps. Make sure you are committed to focus on the goal. Be ambitious to stretch yourself.

Realistic- you have to be genuine about the steps you want to take. This step helps you to think and research more about your goal and see if it is realistic for you to achieve it at that time. Assess if you have the right resources to achieve the goal ie skills, money or time.

Time bound- you need to set time to achieve your goal, otherwise if it is endless goal*. The time specifications will reduce procrastination and lack of motivation. Hence you should be able to know if your steps are for short term or long term goals and what is the specific time set for accomplishing the goal. Is it a year, two years, ten years? Be specific on the timings and the days you are going to engage on the goal and keep a reminder on the phone or in your diary.

Ways of keeping SMART Goals:

Write down the goals on paper and keep the paper in place so you can see them regularly or even daily. Keep the dream alive and remind yourself daily about your dream, aims and objectives. Master the message and sell it to others who can support it. A study in Harvard University indicated that people who write down their goals are highly likely to achieve them more than those who do not.

Position your life in the direction you want to go and remove distractions. Restructure your life to accommodate your goals and vision. Keep the **focus** on your goals and say no to all diversions.

Stay **informed** and surround yourself with **resources** that help your goal i.e. books, seminars, DVD's. Good information will help you accomplish your goals. Join courses that will equip you with **skills and qualifications** that will help you reach your goal. Update your knowledge consistently through continuous research.

Share your goals with other people who can motivate and support you like family, friends or workmates or people in the same field of work that you aspire to get into.

Identify your enemies and keep away from them. These are people who do not believe in your dream and people who try to distract you from your goals. Stay away from naysayers and time wasters.

Anticipate changes, challenges, obstacles, then plan for them. These could be shortage of resources or delays that could be beyond your control. Allow time for the vision to grow because every dream takes longer time than anticipated. Therefore, you have to keep the finisher fighting spirit despite the setbacks.

Join a group of other people doing the same thing. It is important to network and to do it together with others who shares similar interests. Working as part of the team can raise your motivation.

Create a **climate of confidence** around you by speaking and thinking positive even when it's hard. Keep going and believe in your goals. Visualise yourself attaining your goals. Get **good mentors**, who have been in your kind of journey and done it successfully. They will educate you along the way. They can even warn you of the make mistakes that they experienced.

Identify people who inspire you. Find people who are **good role models** and learn from them. Look at all their successes, their hard work and sacrifices like in athletics, politics, academics, and business or in humanitarian work. Read their books, listen to their audio messages, learn from them and get inspired.

Review your goals to monitor progress and to restructure when need be. Reflective thinking helps you to have a true perspective of situation. It also increases you confidence and clarifies the bigger picture for your goal and further helps you to restructure.

If you are a believer, **pray** for your goals and ask others to pray for you.

Reward yourself once goals are achieved to boost your motivation. Remember to always take time to celebrate your accomplishment.

WINNER'S CHARACTER

Talent and charisma can take you up but character will keep you there. Indeed, this has been proven again and again in the world of celebrities, where people with great talents and influence have made poor choices in life that have damaged their positions. This has been observable in the sports world where some winners earned a lot of respect and admiration after their win, however after a few years their integrity has been proved wanting. Indeed, getting their titles stripped off, disappointing their follower and losing respect by their family. Moreover, their careers are destroyed and their finances crumble down. It is very unfortunate that in today's competitive world, most people can do anything to become successful and famous. There is a culture of stepping on others' heads, to get what one wants, however in the end the individual pays for it when exposed. Same lessons have been learnt in the political and business world, also in marriage, where deception for self-gain has been the order of the day. Nevertheless, one can run and try to hide for a while, but not forever. Hence, **integrity** is vital in all you do, despite the cost.

When you have a good character, you are not afraid of being found out. More so, you have peace within. Your success may be gradual and sometimes slower when doing the right things, but in the end it is well earned. Integrity is the key for a noble character. Indeed, being able to do the right things despite the consequences overcoming the enticements around you is vital. Most people value integrity, but not all are able to follow through. Hence, you have to be **resilient** to build on your integrity to protect your career, your relationships and your achievements.

Additionally, when working toward goals and dreams, you have to be ready for tough times. I am sorry to blow-off the success bubble, but this is reality. Big dreams require **strong** people with tough minds and character. Your **patience** and resilience will be tried from time to time on certain areas like discipline, consistency, management, leadership, loyalty and being able accepting bad news whilst remaining positive. **The stronger the challenge the robust the resistant you need to endure, if you want to succeed**. Resist the nemeses of success mentioned earlier in the chapter like procrastination, fear of being wrong or being different, laziness, poor planning etc. Be a problem solver and also a decisive person.

Conversely, you have to **work hard** to get the required skills and information in order to succeed. Most successful people I have met had to work tirelessly going beyond average. They had to do what it takes to succeed even when no one believed in them or in their dreams. Most people who are very successful, had to work two jobs, study and at the same time build their dreams. Eventually when they succeeded, everyone admired their work. But most people were not willing to pay the price of success.

If you want to succeed in your marriage or business or career or in your charity work, you have to be **strong willed** to step out of the boat and do the extraordinary. Then, as you persist in your efforts you will see success eventually coming through your door. The **focus, discipline and optimistic mind-set** are part of the character you have to cultivate every day. Moreover, you have to be able to let go off people in your camp who might be dragging you down. You also have to say no to some engagements in order to stay focussed and committed to the dream.

Sometimes you will fail, or lose money or associations or time, whilst working towards the dream. However, you have to keep focus, be persistent and consistent.

In the midst of these challenges you have to maintain sanity, be able to look strong and focussed. Despite the odds, you have to **humble and respectful** to other people. Indeed, to achieve a dream you can't do it alone, hence you need to identify whom you need as close supporters, role models, mentors and followers. Then again you need to remain true to them at their position. Hence, avoid arrogance, impatience and self-centeredness. For others to support you and follow you, they need to know that you care for them and value them. Indeed to influence them you need to nurture them, listen to them and understand their needs and be able to add value to them. At the same time have boundaries so that you do not lose focus. All this requires time, patience and effort but it adds value to your dreams and visions accomplishment.

Moreover, to go up you need to **let go** of past failures and mistakes. Some people limit their progress by focussing on past hard experiences. One needs to deal with issues that he/she finds hard to let go off professionally, so that you can follow your dreams. Your bad past does not determine your destiny. I have met some people who are very creative and have extra ordinary gifts but their poor upbringing and bad experiences in life have restricted them.

Remember, we can't erase the past, but we can stop it from manipulating our future. As I stated before, **deal with the past** and move on.

Everyone has a story of failure or being let down by other people or by their own mistakes. Even so, our resilience determines whether we are going to remain defeated or if we can dust off the past and work towards a brighter future. The future is bright, keep the focus and enjoy the journey.

Elude all negative characteristics and associations that might block your success in diverse areas of your life. Most of our negative characteristics and habits are learned behaviour which we can unlearn. You can get rid of catastrophic thinking, self-doubt and wrong associations. Aim at building a positive character and exposing yourself to environments that promote a winning character. Believe in your dreams and in your ability to achieve them. Let the people who can help you in, so that you can push ahead.

With extra support by others you can reach the Zone of proximal development (ZDP) derived by Vygotsky (1978). It is the zone we reach in our productivity, while we collaborate with other people who are more knowledgeable than us. We might not reach this level on our own without these people's support. Hence, we need the scaffolding of supportive family, friends and also of good mentors and role models. These people should be able to promote the winner's character in us.

Characteristics we should elude:

Are you one of these? *Evaluate yourself honestly and make changes for success:-*

Idler, bossy, arrogant, drug addicts, lazy, rude, negative, gossiper, never forgives, rebellious, law breakers, judgmental, proud, needy, over-bearing, indecisive and insensitive.

CHAPTER 5. MANAGING STRESS

I once experienced chronic stress at a time I was working full time in a tough environment whilst studying part-time and I was also actively involved in the church. I did not eat well nor rarely rested for a long time. I started to feel weak and experiencing pains in my chest especially during exam times. I recall I went to see my doctor thinking with excruciating pain that had suddenly appeared whilst I was driving on the motorway. Then, my doctor diagnosed it as anxiety attack and advised me to slow down in my life engagements. His advice opened my eyes and I had to restructure my life, reducing engagements. I realised it wasn't worth rushing after endless engagements and in the end get sick as a result. Now, I am happier and very vigilant with my time management and the anxiety problems have disappeared. Anytime I feel like am getting exhausted, I consciously slow down. My encounter helped me to be aware of my own life and it also led me to campaign against 'living stressful lifestyles', which I call running after the wind. **Our health and peace in life are more important than gaining any title, or money, or any fame.**

Are you juggling too much in life and you are feeling exhausted and stressed out? This theme is for you before it is too late. Remember the old saying that *'You can't burn the candle at both ends'.* Nevertheless, today we've gone from candle power to nuclear power, where we are in an infinite ride in search of success, fame, bigger and better things in our life. We want bigger cars, bigger homes, better I-phones, I-pads. We want better paid jobs, better body figures, better families and relationships and the list is endless. However, we forget that each of us has been designed with a restricted ability and time for specific assignments in life. That is why we discussed your purpose and passions in life, to help you stop running around following assignments that are not in your enterprise. **We only have 24 hours in a day and we need to manage our time and resources appropriately**

without burning-out. When there is burn out in any part of our lives, then there is no joy and our confidence is eroded. Hence, our ability to balance is diminished, sapping up our creativity energy distorting our outlook on life in general and our capacity to have a flourished life. Moreover feeling of fatigue embrace our lives and our life gets out of balance and we get stressed with our ways of living.

Stress is termed as mental or emotion tension or strain or suffering. Typically, stress is a result of how we think of situations around us that lead to anxiety. Then our bodies reacts to our thoughts processes. Stress can also be instinctive response to unexpected events known as 'fight or flight'. Stress response can cause physiological changes and if persistence causes psychological and emotional responses too. Acute stress helps us achieve and mobilise resources for example when studying for an exam, whilst chronic stress exhausts all the resources. **Most of us move from acute stress to being chronically stressed due to unhealthy lifestyles which we adopt.**

Unattended chronic stress can lead to anxiety problems and health disorders. Indeed, if stress issues are still not addressed appropriately, they can lead to mental health issues which includes psychotic illnesses ie Depression, Bipolar, Borderline personality disorders, Schizophrenia, PSTD(Post traumatic stress disorder) among others. Physical health problems can also be aggravated if stressful lifestyles are paramount in our lives.

Statistics shows that most of stress issues are work related in Britain, although there are other causes related to lifestyles for example health problems, relationship problems, financial issues among others. UK statistics 2011 showed that 7Million tranquillisers were prescribed for anxiety and this number increases every year. In UK 1 in 20 adults have anxiety problems as reported by(NHS). The Guardian newspaper Nov 2011 reported that 50% Britons fail to sleep due to insomnia issues while the daily telegraph august 2013 reported that there are more admissions in NHS hospitals in 2013 due to stress related issues.

The Kenyan daily nation newspaper August 2013 reported that Kenyans living abroad especially in the USA have been reported to have increased levels of stress resulting to relationship problems, depression and increased rate of suicides. These statistics among others all over the world on STRESS RELATED ISSUES are very alarming!

Indeed, there is no need to go through life stressed out, whilst you can control it. You make your engagements, hence you have power to evaluate and restructure. You can also learn how to manage your finances and relationships. Additionally, you can learn how to attain healthy lifestyles and also how to cope during traumatic times. Hopefully you are ready to take back the control in your life and lessen chronic stress.

Signs of chronic stress:
- Losing self-confidence and motivation.
- Poor/loss of concentration/irrational thoughts.
- Increased irritability and mood swings.
- Loss of appetite.
- Unhappiness, helplessness and hopelessness.
- Poor sleeping patterns /insomnia/cannot switch off.
- Avoiding people/isolation.
- Feelings of agitation and restlessness.
- Feeling utterly tired and always in a rush.
- Physical problems like headaches, indigestions.
- Hard to make decisions.
- Over-eating.
- Lack of interest in sex for married couples.
- Drinking and smoking to cope – indulge in alcohol drugs including prescribed tablets and illegal drugs.
- Feelings of anxiety and tension /anxiety attacks.
- Self-harming, Compulsive disorders, debt crisis, poor time management.
- Depression and suicide ideations.

Key areas of stress management:
- **Time management**
- **Financial management**
- **Harmonizing lifestyles**

TIME MANAGEMENT

Real success is being able to spend your time engaging in productive and meaningful activities like building relationships with family, taking time to study, time to work and invest and also having time to relax and reflect. **Our lives need a balance between our emotional, relational, health, social, and spiritual.** If we spend our time on the wrong things than our success is compromised, since some areas of our lives are suffering and this distress can be detrimental to other areas of our lives. Hence, I believe the time management is an essential skill in life. If we do not manage our time then we lose balance and our life can become chaotic, unhealthy and stressful. Being organised would help us filter our lives the clutter we do not need.

So, what are the most important areas of your life? How much time do you allocate to each of the areas?
Family/marriage
Health-exercise, diet, doctor check-ups
Social/friends/recreation
Work/studies/Business
Faith and spiritual
Rest/sleep/me-time
Recreation time
To me, health, family, faith and work are on the top of the list and I ensure I have allocated enough hours for them every day. Nevertheless, I make sure I have enough time to rest and I also incorporate a bit of social and recreation time every fortnight. Most of us know what is important but we unconsciously lose focus and get carried away by to do lists, like calling a friend. Sometimes the call can take an hour or more, losing time to engage in productive work or in quality family time. Other people can spend a lot of time watching

TV or on the internet or just in the gym and they forget to spend time resting their minds or in engaging with their work or studies. No wonder there are so many projects we start off and never finish them because we never reviewed whether we had time for such activities. Other times relationships are broken because of broken promises like parents being too engaged at work and having less time for their children's ball games or PTA meetings. **Time management is imperative to success and stress reduction.** Indeed, when we are less stressed we are healthy with diminished anxiety disorders and stress issues. However we have to plan and remain disciplined to carry out our time management plan. As Martin Luther King Junior stated *"Human progress is neither automatic nor inevitable... Every step towards the goal requires sacrifice, suffering, and struggle; the tireless exertions and passionate concern of dedicated individuals"*.

You must be ready to actively balance your time in order to reduce stress in your life. Some of the anxiety problems and stress disorder issues are due to our lack of time management. Most of us fit in too much into our schedule, then we spend our time jumping from one thing to another. Sometime, the quality of our work is not good because of the rush. In the end we feel frustrated. However, if we balance our time then we will have to say no to a thousand engagement and focus on the few important one. In the end one is productive, not stressed, and happy with personal achievements.

There is another group of people who revel in procrastinating. They recognise their chores but they wait till the deadline time of the task to start off. Hence, they work in a rush and their concentration is pushed by their fear to meet deadline. These individuals find it very intense if something goes not according to plan, for example if one has a report to write and hand in within two hours and then the computer crushes or they are called into an emergency meeting leaving them with no time to complete their task. Then panic sets in and confusion overrules. Most times these individuals are aware of the task at hand weeks before, but they do not bother to do it when they have time. If you find yourself in this list, it is time to try and make changes.

When you do your duties on time then you have time to rest and even time to review your work. I once worked in a hospital where the Multidisciplinary meetings were on Monday morning and all departments needed to present the previous week's reports. Most colleagues did not summarize their work the week before and they were always tensed on Monday mornings. Others preferred to call in sick on Monday mornings to avoid the meeting I presumed, but they could have coincidentally fallen sick most of the Mondays. Still, others handed in the wrong reports which had been changed dates but not the contents. You could call this fraud, but besides they managed to embarrass themselves when they were found out. In the same team, I met very intelligent and organised people who completed their reports the week before and on Monday morning they briskly walked into the meeting confidently because they had managed their work and time well.

I hope you are one of the confident and organised people, who finish their tasks on time. By being a team player and sharing work equally for successful completion. Aim to divide your weekly and daily hours to plan your time. **Evaluate the hours you spend on important engagements**. Review areas which you need to make changes; for example you might be wasting a lot of time shopping, you can make it a weekly task instead of daily task or you can spend less time on the phone chatting and make quality time for family. Also maybe you need more time off in order to follow your personal goals.

You should aim to work effectively, enjoying your relationships and having time to rest, re-energize and avoid time wasting on unimportant things.

Use a similar pie-chart to assess your weekly time allocation:

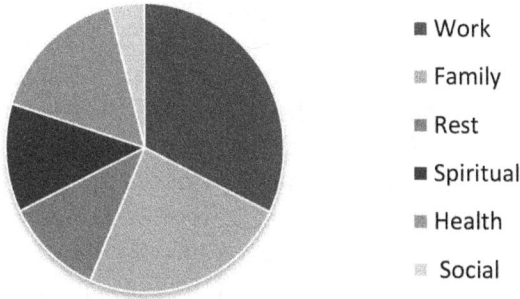

- ▪ Work
- ▦ Family
- ▪ Rest
- ▪ Spiritual
- ▦ Health
- ▨ Social

FINANCIAL MANAGEMENT

Most people in our world today are stressed due to financial problems. Statistics show that financial issues are great stressor for many and are number one reason for many divorces. **Some of us are good at budgeting whilst others are sucked into the culture of spending beyond our means.** John Maxwell stated that *'The secret of your success is determined by your daily agenda ...we over exaggerate yesterday and over-estimate tomorrow and we under-estimate today'*.

If you look around your city, there is always a sale going on. It's either New Year's sales, then Easter sales, then summer sales, then autumn sales, then Christmas sale. But have you ever wondered why sales all year round? It is a way to entice you to buy whatever you do not need. Most of us buy items we never use and then complain of lack of money and also lack of space in our wardrobes for women while our men's garages and stores are packed. So, what is your current financial status?

If you are struggling with your finances, do not wallow in guilt or avoid your bills. Instead, do something to change your circumstances. Start by going through your bills and income, ascertaining how much you owe and how much you have paid. Then, make a good budget plan and stick to it. If you find it difficult to reconcile your finances, ask for assistance from people who offer assistance. There are some free government and charitable financial advisers who can offer you support.

When you are offered financial support, take it and put it into practice. I will give you some simple tips of how to overcome debt. But first step it to **aim at spending less than you earn**. Never use credit cards on perishables but for emergencies and pay them back promptly. Practice paying for items in cash which reduces aimless spending. Also try to carry food from home or to eat before leaving home. This reduces overspending on buying coffees and muffins all over the place. You might wonder how many coffees can lead you to debt, but look at it this way. If you buy a coffee and a muffin every day for at least six days a week, how much will you have spent in a year? Was it necessary? I do not think so.

Most offices I have worked in or even visited offer you coffee and tea, so why do you need to have Starbucks coffee every day and remain in debt. Make it a one off treat, maybe in the weekend or on a day out with friends. When you reduce your spending on little stuff like coffee, eating out, impulse buying, you will be surprised by how quick you will pay off your debts. Moreover, you will be able to save for important investments like mortgage down payments, or capital for a business, or savings for retirement.

When you are able to stick to a budget, then you are able to make conscious financial plans and decisions that will work for you. Then, you will have financial freedom and rarely worry of being repossessed, or losing your relationships, or assets due to debt issues. You will also be able to plan for your holidays and pay for them up-front. I have come across some adverts on TV, affirming that you can go on holiday and pay for it three years after. And I wonder why anyone would do that, with the current financial climate of recession. What if you were made redundant in the next few years with all the accumulated debt and no savings? You will not only hurt yourself but also those who are close to you.

So I will insist, do not live beyond your means, keep a budget and ask for financial advice or accountant help in your business. It is better to be safe than sorry.

Tips on money management;
- Take stock of your current financial status.
- Work for regular income.
- Stop borrowing.
- Record and monitor your expenditure.
- List your debts.
- Make a strategic plan to repay your debts.
- Pay your debts following a good plan.
- Look for good advice and counsel.
- Be content with what you have.
- Deal with bad habits like gambling, impulsive buying.
- Budget your income consistently.
- Change your habits like using credit card, pay cash and if you do not have save for it.
- Save at least 10% of your income regularly.
- Spend at most 80% of your income.
- Invest for future.
- For Christians –tithe10% and pray for God's wisdom and guidance
- Have good role models-because one surest way to succeed at something is to spend time with the person who has done just that.
- Nurture others into good financial management like your children, friends and family.
- Attend financial management courses or seminars-Prov19;2 says that 'one should listen to advice and accept instructions and he/she will be wise'.
- Be generous by meeting other peoples' needs especially the needy and the poor.
- Do not deal with doorstep sellers or doorstep money lenders, check the APR% rate.
- Avoid business and purchase contracts that do not serve you fairly.

HARMONIZING LIFESTYLES

Being calm, composed and in control helps us to succeed in various settings, boosting our confidence, productivity, health and happiness. Hence, resting, recreation time and relaxation are indispensable in life. However most of us live chaotic lives, which includes working endlessly without breaks unless we are away on holidays. Some people even when they go on holidays, they still carry their laptops and books with them and they keep their mobiles on to keep in touch with the world they have gone to rest from. I wonder what would happen if you switched your mobile off for two weeks whilst on holiday. I know the only difference is that you will rest your mind, rejuvenate, and have time to re-think better ways to approach life. Indeed, in presence of quietness, there is peace and creativity. Hence we should all aim for quietness in life but we have to work hard to dislodge all the distractions in our lives including TV, radio, Ipads, mobile phones. I have nothing against gadgets since they are necessary, but they should have a time and a place. Our time to rest our mind and refresh to maintain serenity should be important as well.

Most of our psychological, physical and spiritual difficulties are due to lack of relaxation and resting time. Our bodies and minds are always on the go and in the end their energy is choked. We all need to consciously take time out to relax and refresh, if we do not want to become prey to problems like anxiety disorders, heart problems among others. You can take time to listen to good music or meditate or pray. Going out for a nature walk in the park is very healthy and relaxing. One can also take time to go for a swim or to write a poem, **engaging in whatever you enjoy to do in order to relax.** Take time to do things that take your mind and body from usual chores and environments. Some people can spend a whole day trying to solve a technical problem, whilst another person would just have a break and walk the dog down the park and when they get back to work they are fresh to face the problem. The person who took time out will be more productive and less stressed. Indeed, the person will find it easier to get along with the people around, because there is less exhaustion and irritation. As a matter of fact most marriages fail due to sex problems which are related to stress and exhaustion. **Lack of time for creativity and life management problems can overflow, causing poor intimacy**

and conflicts in relationships. If these issues are not resolved promptly other areas of life will get affected instigating marriage problems, financial crisis and healthy problems and depression. Hence, it is vital to take time out to rest, reflect and re-energize.

Most people are burning the candle of life from both sides, hence they are always feeling frustrated and exhausted. The world is on the go 24/7, however you have control over your choices and time plans. The time I suffered from anxiety due to overworking and I queried within myself, whether if I died the world would stop. The truth was, it would not have stopped even for a second. Then, why should we allow ourselves to never have a breather and we keep running after things that have no reverence relevance? for our lives. Your job, company, associates would continue normally, even though you were not there. Hence, it is paramount to respect your body and your serenity by often taking time out to rest and to re-energize. You will even be a happier and healthier person when you have refreshed.

Additionally, managing your health and balancing your time is a vital skill for life management. As pointed earlier in the chapter you need to take time to draw a time plan that strikes a balance between your relationships, your work, rest time, house chores, exercise and recreation time. Making sure you take a review of your time plan regularly to avoid over-commitment which can lead to exhaustion and anxiety. Good goal setting and budgeting helps us to manage life objectives. Decent budgeting reduces financial strain that can envelope your life if care is not taken. Moreover maintain a healthy diet and good exercise is paramount. Furthermore positive thinking, talking and association reduce low self-esteem and social conflicts. It also increases hope, productivity and further helps an individual to build good relationships and associations that compliments one's life.

Our living conditions should be conducive for our health, inner peace and serenity. Avoid living in noisy areas or areas which are crowded with poor living conditions like lighting, ventilation, poor amenities and infrastructure. Stay away from areas that have high pollution and insecurity.

Living in these un-conducive neighbourhoods will not only affect your physical health but also your emotional and mental health. Some of the people living in these conditions are as a result of poverty, but once the individual has managed to stabilise the earnings, it is important to seek for better living conditions. I have come across well paid people living in areas which are noisy and polluted, just because they are familiar with the areas. Eventually, their environment affects their health including problems like asthma, cancer and anxiety problems. Aim to have a good earning to be able to live in comfortable conditions. Sometimes if you searched for housing outside the city you might find a good house in a country side with the same amount of rent you pay in the inner city. However, you will be looking after your mental and physical health conditions reducing stress. Therefore, all these areas of regimes intertwine with each other, indicating that for one to be successful, healthy and happy, we need to learn the skills, make good decisions and harmonise our lifestyles.

Procrastination is a thief of your success, happiness and health. Hence, you have to make a decision to deal promptly with life challenges. Unattended life issues like psychological, emotional, relationship, financial and health issues can cause stress in our lives. As a result, it is important to ask for help promptly for example whilst dealing with bereavement, divorce, redundancy or low self-esteem. Problems solve the issues and do not try to sweep the issue under the carpet, avoidance will only make your life more stressful. Look for professional counsel in difficult and complicated issues and aim to deal with them effectively and promptly with the support available.

WAYS OF ORGANIZING LIFE

- Use of good problem solving skills and making wise life decisions.
- Learning good coping skills that build resilience during life challenging times
- Using effective relaxation techniques i.e. listening to cool and calming music, deep breathing, having a bubble bath,

having a warm coffee/tea and drinking water.

- Positive self-expressing through journal writing, drawing, singing and painting.
- Sharing your concerns with supportive people and a good cry if you can.
- Going for a walk, exercising and getting a massage.
- Engaging in exciting and enjoyable hobbies like baking, watching comedies, golf, gardening.
- Having a good night sleep and eating a balance diet always.
- Prayer and meditation and taking time out to rest, refresh and reflect.
- Distracting negative thoughts through positive self-talk, helpful association and engagements.
- Dealing with stressful issues promptly and living in healthy neighbourhoods.
- Avoiding destructive behaviours, habits and associations.
- Forgiving and compromising with others' weaknesses and letting go of own mistakes.
- Having a good time out - dancing, walking, surfing etc.

CHAPTER 6. FINDING HOPE, FAITH AND HAPPINESS

BUILDING HOPE AND FAITH

A decade ago, I became acquainted to two ladies who became my good friends. Both ladies had known each other for a long time and had gone through life together. One of the ladies whom I will call Jackie had a young daughter. She was going through a divorce and was in her third year of her degree studies. The other lady whom I will call Susan for confidentiality was heavily pregnant, jobless and single, since she had just been abandoned by her ex-boyfriend. As I got to know both ladies better, I realised they were very different in the way they viewed life. Jackie was very positive and she hoped to succeed in life. All she talked about was finishing her studies, getting through the divorce and meeting someone to marry again, which I found peculiar. Indeed, to my surprise within a short time she had finished her degree and started working and was now actively going out to meet prospective partners. I was fascinated by her enthusiasm and hope in life, despite her previous predicaments. On the other hand, Susan was so disconsolate, since she had not finished her studies, she was single, jobless and expectant. She tried to pursue her ex-boyfriend with no avail. With time, Susan's situation got worse and she became very depressed and we advised her to go back to her parents' home. Meanwhile, I moved out of that city, but I kept in touch with both ladies. After five years Jackie had met a nice guy, got married and moved on, living happily and successfully. In the interim, Susan was still living with her parents, she never got a job and was not in a relationship. Her parents took care of her needs and that of her baby's. My two friends' attitudes towards life opened my eyes. Indeed, I realise that **the way you perceive** your circumstances and your future, will navigate the route course that your life takes. If you perceive life as an endless list of struggles then it will be, if you have hope for things to get better, then they will get better. Undeniably, setbacks and challenges come to all of us, but our attitude towards them determines our passage.

Hope is the predictor of our future and it gives us strength to keep going in life. *'You can't have a better tomorrow if you are thinking about yesterday all the times'* as stated by Charles Kettering. True freedom in life is not letting your yesterday affect your today, because what you were is not what you are and not what you will be in the future. **The power is within your perceptions and the choices you take.** You have to choose to move through life valuing yourself, your time, opportunities and influences. Moreover, living without fear, guilt or regret, but enjoying where you are and hoping that it will get better.

Every season in our life is important, whether good, hard or bad. Indeed, it is during hard and tough times when character is shaped and great talents shines. We **learn through failures, mistakes and achievements** and we have hope that things will not always remain the same. This hope makes people fight against injustice or fight for good courses and changes in life. With hope some people are able to change their life conditions, their family and even their community circumstances. However where there is no hope, people stop fighting and pursuing dreams. They become complacent, lazy, bored, depressed and eventually rust out. Your life has to count, not just to you but also to those around you. Do not leave a legacy of giving up, but a legacy of hope and of living life to the full despite the challenges.

Another kind of hope that is valuable is hope in a supernatural power-GOD. Most of us have ignored the spiritual part of our life just because we feel to be in control. However, when we ignore our spiritual being part, then we have a self-inflicted disability in our lives. Although not all people have abandoned the spiritual side of life, some have, while others are ignorant or deceived. Nonetheless, the effects of lack of hope and faith are evident in our day to day living. A study in the University of Miami indicated that **people with a faith are more contented in life and recover quicker** even when facing health ailments or life predicaments. This observation has been seconded by other researchers. They are able to play their part in life and leave the rest to God. They have expectation that God will make ways where there are no ways, beyond their strength. Indeed, most of these people come back and testify how faith got them through rough times and how new doors in their lives opened. Sceptics would argue that they were just lucky, but for me as a Christian, I believe that faith works. I do not want to push my faith down your throat but what I would tell you is that it has worked for me. Indeed, I am not sure where I would be if I had no faith in God for example, when I worked in various mental health Units which were very volatile, at times patients could become very aggressive. Some patients could become malicious and accuse staff of anything and put the staff career and life on the line. I saw some colleagues being sued, or being disciplined, or sometimes being assaulted. But for the decade I worked in mental health, no patient ever laid a finger on me, nor ever accused me of anything. Despite of being professional and respectful to all, I believe my prayer to God for protection every day worked for me. Furthermore, I realised most incidents happened when I was off duty, which made me believe that this was God's protection.

I have met a lot of people who never had any faith but gave accounts of going through life feeling empty on the inside. Despite their success and achievements and having a lot of people around them, until they asked God to help them. I once listened to a gentleman who narrated how successful he was, but his family had lost one of their children in an accident. This tragedy was too much to bear for his family. Even so, his wife found faith and she suddenly became stronger, while he remained angry, in grief and he did not want anything to do with God. But one day he decided to visit his wife's church and for the first time in a long while, he felt a sense of peace in his heart when he said a prayer. Since then, he found faith and the grief and anger slowly disappeared. This man was a very successful person but was suffering on the inside trying to be in control, but it was not until he let go and chose to trust in God that he found peace and hope again.

Many like this man have been carrying burdens in their lives but they are afraid to let go, so as not to look weak. However, having faith is not a sign of weakness but of strength. **Faith strengthens your outlook on life and helps you face challenges.** Prayers help you calm down and relax because you believe in someone stronger than you, who take control of your situation. Nevertheless, having faith doesn't mean that all your life issues are wiped out. No, it just means that the situations do not control your life. You are able to enjoy your life and having a hope that the predicaments will pass on and a new season will come your way. When you have faith and hope you are also able to follow your dreams and action your plans. Faith as described in the book of Hebrews in the bible is the substance of things hoped for, the **confidence that what we hope for, will actually happen.** Hence, it gives us assurance about things we cannot see. As a result of faith, we are able to aim to have healthy lifestyles and good relationships. Moreover, we are able to work towards our dreams and goals, hoping that one day we will get the right results. Without faith in our dreams and in life, we cannot take the right steps and life challenges can overwhelm us. However, hope and faith gives us the motivation to keep going. Hence do not lose faith along the way, encourage yourself even in harsh seasons.

As you might have noticed in other chapters, I have appreciation and respect for science. I believe we need medicines, engineers, neural scientists, psychologists, therapists and other professionals. However, we still need our spirituality and we cannot dispense it to uptake science. I am surprised by how much our society disregard religion, but we are quick to run to church to get married or to be christened and we furthermore want to get buried by a vicar once we have passed on. Yet, when the church stands for what it believes we are ready to criticise it and dismiss its' use. Without being political, I wish you would try faith in God for your own life and for your family if you haven't yet. Without faith and hope peoples' spiritual lives are empty. Then, **they try to fill spiritual emptiness with pleasure using sex, music, drugs, pornography, gambling, and alcohol among other things that at times becomes destructive.** I have nothing against having fun but I wish most of us would seek to have faith. Then our lives would be well balanced since we are spiritual beings. Having come from Africa where most people believe in God I have seen hope in the eyes of many in desperate circumstances. One Friend articulated to me that faith is a clutch, but I think it is a better clutch than drugs, alcohol or other means we use to fulfil our empty spiritual lives. For example have you ever wondered why people in the rich western countries have high rates of depression, anxiety problems, divorces and people committing suicide? Whilst some hungry and malnourished kids in developing world never contemplate committing suicide but they stay together with their families trying their best to survive against all odds?

Conversely, it is because most of the people in impoverished countries have **faith and hope**. I know this because I witnessed it in 1996 January when I volunteered with Light force International UK charity, working with children in North Uganda in the IDP camps. Despite having grown up in Africa, the state and conditions I saw were beyond my imagination and I was overwhelmed. The Lou's in North Uganda had been driven out of their land by the rebels and they had been refugees for over 20 years. Most of them had been killed, while the survivors lived in very impoverished conditions. They did not have beds, they slept on the floor and they had neither food nor water. Most children suffered from malnutrition and from other diseases like scabies, HIV among others. Even at that time, most were still being attacked and killed by rebels, despite the heavy presence of government army in the region. In that moment, I felt hopeless and I wondered what I was doing there since my contribution seemed insignificant.

A memorable incident during my stay was when I visited one of the refugee camps where I witnessed the whole village sharing one big pot of boiled meat, which had been donated by a politician. They were so excited, it seemed like Christmas came early. But to me the pot of meat was just enough to feed 20 people, but there were more than a hundred people waiting for it. Even so, these people hoped that one day, the war will end and they will be able to go back to their land. They asked me to help them and at that moment I was not sure what I could do, but I promised them I will let the people back in UK know of their needs. Since then till now I still advocate for people to sponsor children living in poverty in that region and other parts of the world. However, the lesson I learnt from Ugandans was to remain hopeful in life, seeing beyond hard situations. Moreover to be grateful of what I have at present and to stop complaining over small issues.

Indeed, there is always someone in a worse situation than you. If this community in refugee camps could have faith and hope, so can you despite your predicaments.

Reflect on **how your faith and hope in life is today. How are you looking at your present circumstances?** Let the situations not define your life but see them as seasonal, build your hope and faith. Tomorrow will be a better day.

REALITY ABOUT HAPPINESS

During my undergraduate studies in psychology, I did a small scale study on what happiness means and how people evaluate happiness in their lives. My participants came from different parts of the world and their outlook on happiness was very interesting. Some of the participants **perceived happiness to be embodied to current situations and events**. Hence, one gets happy when the situation is favourable to them and when their current expectations are met. This could be for example passing an exam or winning a lottery or through hearing a funny joke or achieving something like getting married or giving birth or buying a new house. Their happiness brought joy and sense of fulfilment, nevertheless it appeared to be short lived when the situation or event effect wore off. This kind of happiness was also connected with materialism of trying to get stuff which will make one feel happy, for example buying fancy cars, living in flashy neighbourhoods and attending parties and building careers to earn a lot of money. Indeed, this kind of **success brings happiness and comfort in life and it is situated to time and events**. However, this kind of happiness can be short lived if other areas of life are not well integrated and balanced.

Some of the participants in my small scale study viewed happiness as a way of life shared with close family members and friends. An Asian participant recalled how he enjoyed the time he spent with his family chatting away with other males sitting in a corner of the estate, while the ladies in the family stayed in the kitchen cooking and also sharing stories, talking and laughing, as the kids were playing outside. To him this kind of life brought good memories, joy and happiness. Indeed, his **happiness was influenced by the possession of good relationships including family and friends and sharing life together**. Ultimately, all participants agreed there was a dilemma of what true happiness is. However, they all acknowledged that the lifestyles we choose can bring happiness and the kind of relationships we nurture can affect our fulfilment in life. Indeed, the study supported Prof Selingman positive psychology interpretation that happiness can be assimilated through learning to be satisfied with what we have.

Even so, most of us proclaim our aim to be happy when we reach our dreams. For example, when we get our dream career, or when we marry the right person, or if we go on holiday, or when we win the lottery, but what does happiness really mean? What happens if we get the girl or the money? Do we remain happy or does our happiness wear off with time? It is important to live comfortably and to achieve the things we need in our life which makes life more comfortable. Hence meeting our needs are vital and also being able to follow our dream which gives us a sense of achievement which conveys contentment.

Nevertheless, pleasure and contentment only lasts in us when we have stability within ourselves. Hence, **most of our happiness is found within us, but not externally**. The external situations enhance what is within. Indeed, real happiness comes from you being able to choose the right attitude in any given setting, despite the circumstances. True happiness comes when you can control your feelings and thoughts on different issues, remaining calm and positive. The ability to choose positive attitude is a result of good self-esteem, where self-worth and confidence is not determined by the circumstances or by other people's views. You then have the ability to value your life and your choices and remain steady most of the time. Unfortunately, the people who put their ego first in their circumstances, when they are faced by challenges their true confidence and self-worth is eroded. Hence, their happiness changes with circumstances. One scholar said that the only constant variable in life is change hence we have to learn how to handle changes in life. Otherwise our self-worth, mood and attitudes will be swayed away every time changes occurs. Hence, it is important to work on your self-esteem and enhance your ability to remain calm in all conditions. Indeed, most strong and calm people are valued and respected in our society because they are able to be steady. Without a doubt, people even trust them to be leaders since they have managed their attitudes and behaviour. More so, most people looking for long term connections usually look for people who are stable, positive and happy in their own lives, hoping those characteristics will remain constant during their relationship.

Overall, everyone deserves happiness and it is within one's grasp. Hence you need to evaluate how you feel about yourself most of the time. Have you ever noticed that sometimes you can just get angry without talking to anyone, or you can be watching TV and suddenly you feel angry. What happens? It is the thoughts you entertain in your mind that influence your feelings. **So, do you feel happy and contented with your life or do you feel unhappy and sad most of the times?**

If your feel low in mood, sad and unhappy, then it is crucial for you to evaluate what makes you feel that way. Most times our thoughts and talks shape how we feel. Hence, it is important to check the thoughts we entertain in our mind most of the times. If there are **thoughts of guilt, or anger, or of low-esteem or offence and resentment, then you have to deal with them effectively and promptly.**

These patterns are usually learned behaviour which can be challenged and changed. So if you are willing to face head on your mood, thoughts and negative behaviour talks and association, this will be productive to enhancing your feelings of happiness. Most of us have been hurt by other people and we carry-on offended. These feelings of offence and anger brood slowly and affect our outlooks and mood. Hence, it is important to deal with issues promptly because they not only affect our mood but our health too, both mental health but also physically health and spiritual health as well. According to neural scientist Dr Caroline leaf, negative thoughts trigger toxins that affect our bodies negatively and eventually result to ill health. She further ascertained that **90% of physical diseases in human live are connected to their negative thought life.** Without a doubt with this kind of thought issues and health problems then our happiness is eroded. Therefore, it is vital for all to manage our thoughts and if there are any negative recurring thoughts and feelings that are challenging to get rid of by **seeking help from a counsellor or a therapist.** Also aim to forgive people who offend you and avoid retaining resentment.

Remember, boats only sink when storms on the outside get on the inside. So, your happiness will only diminish when life situations get into your thoughts, speech and actions. Hence, take control of your mind and self-esteem, and seek assistance where need be.

Moreover, when we are happy on the inside then we are able to make good choices in our lives. We are also able to get along with other people hence our social lives are enriched. Indeed, our marriages and relationships are strengthened, when we are calmer, forgiving and supportive with each other. Hence, maintaining good social relations is vital to our happiness. Some people run after careers and money and they enjoy the thrill of achievement but sometimes they lose their close relations and end up lonely. Therefore, it is vital **to cultivate good relationships with your family and friends,**

especially those who are confidants. Take the effort to input into their lives and one day when you need them they will be there for you. Most people when they are in their death bed do not care about how many houses or cars they bought, or how much money they earned. What makes most people feel their lives were well lived is determined by the people around them and the significant difference they made in other people's lives. People come to the death bed because the person was there for them in time of need. Besides, it is not only when we are needed that people matter, but it throughout our lives as we interact.

Although it is important to be self-sufficient, it is also valuable to create good memories by sharing good times with people who are close to you. Indeed, most children when they grow up they rarely recall the money their parents spent on them, but what remains in their recollected memories are the valuable times they spent with their parents. The Christmas times, the camping's, the ball games, the swimming contests, all the events and activities they shared. These events and relationships bring fulfilment to individuals' life. Especially, when they are good times they are recounted as happy times. **That is why we hear some people say they had a happy childhood while others didn't have such. Parents need to try their best and create happy environment** for their children to grow in. As established by psychologists, childhood experiences shape people's lives, hence it is vital to be keen on the environments we expose our children to. Moreover, the nurturing and care that we give to the children should be of high standard. I once listened to a TV interview of an American celebrity, who was asked to share his childhood memories. The celebrity said that his childhood was lonely because he was a lone child and his parents being both Hollywood actors, who were always working away from home. As a result, this individual grew up in a big house with nannies and a lot of material stuff, but with less recollection of sharing time with his mum and dad. Hence, he learnt to entertain himself and ended up keeping company with the wrong crowd as a teenager. Although he was reformed in the time of his interview and was doing well in his career and married with a son, he vowed to always be there for his kids since he did not want a repeat of his parents' mistakes. This TV interview highlights the need for good quality time within families.

Moreover as adults, it is our responsibility to **expose ourselves to positive environments.** Our **choices of associations, our career and living conditions should enhance our inner peace and serenity.** When you are at peace within, you have a feeling of fulfilment, stability and happiness. Furthermore, ailments outlined earlier in the book due to stressful lifestyles will not come near you. Hence, you have to **maintain healthy lifestyles** quantified in the book like good diet, exercise, good sleeping patterns, time and financial management, having time out to relax and for recreation among others. All these inputs will help you have a happier life as outlined further down.

RIP-OFFS TO HAPPINESS IN LIFE

Most of the areas discussed in this book are significant to our happiness. If they are not attended the joy of our life is deprived. Here are examples of joy stealers;

Conflicts, erroneous thinking, self-hatred, anger, stress, Loss, loneliness, depression, discomfort, life crisis , burn-out, being judgmental, fear, guilt, rejection, frustration, tiredness, poor self-image, isolation, addictions, consistent complaining, jealousy, hopelessness and anxiety.

RECOMMENDATIONS FOR ACHIEVING HAPPIER LIFE

- **Cultivating good self-esteem.** Enjoying and accepting who you are and not comparing yourself.
- **Letting go of offenses**- people will offend you, but you have to learn to forgive and let go.
- **Establishing good relationships** is significant. Memories and time spent with others brings joy in life.
- **Going after your dreams** helps you feel accomplished in life. Build confidence in your gifts, talents and opportunities, then maximise your potential.
- **Choosing a good environment to live and work in.** Avoid toxic environments which erode your happiness affecting your mental and physical health critically.

- **Dealing with issues of life promptly and effectively.** Seek help where need be.
- **Helping others** brings joy and happiness to them and to us. Aim to help someone every day.
- **Healthy lifestyles cultivate peace,** health and happiness i.e. good diet, sleep, exercise, time and financial management etc.
- **Being grateful** of our current life success and achievement. Seeing good in the present and having hope for a good future. Avoid complaining and enjoy things and people in your life.
- **Having fun and creating good memories** with family and friends like camping, holidays, parties etc.
- **Challenging negative thinking.** By disengaging from destructive behaviours, talks and associations at all times.
- **Smiling and laughing** more often.
- **Awakening your spirituality, faith and hope**.
- **Enjoying nature** by taking time out and walking through the woods, or walking by the riverside or having a picnic outside or watching the stars at night.
- **Overcome consumer mentality** where our joy is drawn by what we buy and possess.
- **Trying new adventures** like travelling, mountain climbing gives you time out and also time for reflecting and re-energizing. When we are tired, bored and exhausted we are irritable and our happiness fades.
- **Building resilience**- through learning skills that helps you survive and thrive through life situations.

MARKS OF HAPPINESS

- Self-awareness and contentment with self.
- Relaxed mood, joyful, smiling and laughter.
- Enthusiasm in life, hopeful, optimistic.
- Mindful of present with no distractions by worry, guilt and concerns.
- Forgiveness and inner peace.
- Socializing and acceptance of others
- Resilient, assertive, persistence and tolerant.

- Positive mind-sets and sincere.
- Healthy relationships and positive associations.
- Healthy lifestyles.
- Gratefulness of life and enjoyment.
- Compassion and being helpful to others.

CHAPTER 7. MAINTAINING THE WHOLE
ITALIAN LESSON

Italy was ranked among the top ten countries of the world for having quality of life by the World Healthy Organisation (2000). Having visited the country several times and mingled with Italians, as I summarise my book I want to share practical life lessons from Italy. Even though every country has its good points and areas that require improvement, as an advocate for happy healthy living, I am obliged to share my insight on the subject from Italians. My comprehension is enhanced through experience, having been married for a few years to a gorgeous, loving Italian man and having socialized with his friends and family. Even so, I do not write this article to please my husband or my in-laws, but I do it for us to learn more practically where to improve in our lives as we attain healthy, happier and successful lifestyles.

    1. **FAMILY BASED**- Italians are very family oriented. Everything and all occasions are shared among family members and friends. Most families talk more than twice a week, despite the distance between them. Most children stay at home until they get good education and a good job and are supported by their parents all through. When the parents are old, the children take care of their parents willingly. This family tie gives identity and stability. The individuals' self-esteem is enhanced through love and support received from those close to them. Unlike most other communities who have lost value for family ties and moved into individualism which eventually leads to loneliness and depression. It is important for each of us to belong, hence it is vital to build good family and social relationships.

    2. **RELAXED LIFESTYLES**- Italians are not rushed by life like most of the other countries in the developed world. They enjoy at least 1-2 months summer holidays, for those who can afford they spend 3 months of summer breaks every year near the beach taking activities like swimming, cycling

and also enjoying time with family and friends. This lifestyle helps their bodies, minds and relationships to flourish. They have siestas every afternoon in the hot season. Am not sure about their pockets though, since most of their businesses are closed during these times, but they still seem to get back okay. They seem to value their time out which pays off eventually in their long healthy life which is filled with joy, happiness and good memories.

3. **RELIGIOUS**- 95% of Italians are Catholics. Although, most people do not go to church regularly, most of family occasions are religious based. They value christening of children, church weddings and church funerals. They believe in life after death. Their belief in God helps them stay calm and put their trust in God. Most mothers pray for their families constantly and if you are a believer like me you know there is power of a praying parent. Their spiritual belief in God gives them stability in their life, there is no place for emptiness to be filled by drugs, alcohol and sex. Faith as ascertained earlier is indispensable for fulfilled living.

4. **SELF EXPRESSIVE**- Whether happy or upset, Italians do not reserve their true feelings. They show full joy and express themselves happily. When sad and upset, they do not beat around the bush either. As a result, less depression is apparent among them, since emotions suppression and repression is reduced. Appropriate self-expression promotes good relationships and great mental and physical health. Indeed, Italians live longer and healthier.

5. **ORGANIC FOOD**- It is hard to find McDonald's, Subways and all other junk food shops in Italy. Most Italian foods are organic and healthy. They eat good food all the time. I am not sure there are cases of eating disorders apparent in other countries like obesity and anorexia. Italian food is known all over the world and most of it is prepared with healthy Olive oil. They enjoy eating their food and they have a siesta after the meal.

6. **CULTURE and EDUCATION**- Italians have reserved their culture. This helps them have self-identity and promotes self-esteem. The culture, history and the good weather has made Italy a destination for many tourists from all over the

world, promoting their economy. The culture promotes the importance for education and most parents support their children to study till they get first degree. Some individuals have taken advantage of their parents and wasted a lot of time in colleges and universities. Nonetheless, their parents' dreams is to have educated and successful generations who have a sense of responsibility to endeavour and achieve their dreams which makes life more meaningful.

Conclusively, Italians inspire me to aim to balance my life between family, faith, rest, healthy living and education as I follow my dreams and enjoy my life. I hope we can all learn something from Italy and put it into practice. Like Thomas Edison noted "Opportunity is missed by most people because it is dressed in overalls and looks like work." Let us not miss the opportunity to make changes in our life to gain health happiness and success. We live once, there is no time for rehearsal, thus it is vital to maximise our potential and to enjoy every point of our lives. We are all capable of having a healthy happy and successful life.

HALF-FULL PERCEPTION

Anais Nin stated that *'Life shrinks or expands in proportion to one's courage'.* Therefore, you have to encourage yourself through life when you face setbacks. Life can be a bed of roses with great times which are accompanied by challenges which are the thorns in a rose. Hence, you have to learn to handle the thorns if you need to enjoy the smell of roses in your life. I wish I could tell you that setbacks in life won't come to you when you apply all the tips outlined, but I would be lying. Life storms will come to all of us, but the difference is in our preparedness. Being proactive with knowledge is helpful and moreover putting into practice the skills we have acquired is obligatory. I have observed that every step of life has its' challenges, no matter how glamorous it seems. The higher you go the stronger the challenges. Hence, it is important to be realistic and ready to overcome.

The secret of life is to enjoy where you are, on your way to your destiny. The journey process comes with good, happy and hard times, but you have to embrace all, stay strong and keep going. If you look hard enough, there are good things in your life today. Moreover, there is always someone in worse situation than you. Look at the orphans and the refugees. Are you in such conditions as them? I bet not. So, look closely to what you have and start to enjoy it. Look for opportunities to solve other people's problems and then, there are opportunities for you to get a job, or to meet someone, or to get the experience you need or the advice and knowledge you need. If there are areas you need assistance, never hesitate to ask for help. But then again remember destructive behaviour will not help your situation, but it will only destroy your life, hence keep away from them

The glass in life is always half full, so it is important to learn how to handle challenges and be able to enjoy life. No matter how big our failures or challenges or mistakes are, we can get through them over time if we get the right support. There are no rehearsals in life, so if you waste your life being depressed, or complaining, or in self-pity, you waste the potential and opportunity to make a decent legacy. **Aim to maximise your gifts, talents and opportunities.**

Keep learning and practicing what you learn daily as you follow your dreams. Remember character may be manifested in great moments, but it is made in small ones, so do not dispense small beginnings. The process will make you strong, wiser and eventually usher you to destiny, nonetheless enjoy the process.

Remember, where there is a will there is a way and whatever is beyond your ability, say a prayer and leave it in God's hands. There will be issues that are beyond your control but do not let them swallow your passions, energy opportunities and talents.

Do not give up, when you lose in life, dare to dream and start again. Most successful and happy people are those who have risen over setbacks, identified their opportunities in life and learnt to maximise their potential as they enjoy their everyday life.

I hope that you live a happy, healthy and successful life and moreover help others as you go through life. Additionally being able to handle good and hard times, always seeing the glass as half full but not half empty.

DREAMS COME TRUE, FOLLOW THEM.

As I conclude this book I would like to share with you **the journey to my dreams**. Primarily, I had a good childhood, having been born in a middle class Kenyan family. My dad was a Presbyterian Minister and he also went on to be a tutor, a lecturer and also a farmer at different points of his life. My mum was a school teacher, a church elder and a great mother. I was the first born and the only girl in my family, with two younger sibling brothers. I had been born in Scotland (UK) whilst my dad pursued his two Masters' degrees in Theology at the University of ST Andrews, but I was raised in central Kenya, on the beautiful slopes of Mount Kenya.

Our home was in a lovely farm ranch, where I have great memories of growing up, especially the great times with friends and neighbours playing hide and seek in the village farms. I also enjoyed picking coffee in our farm, milking cows and growing different horticultural crops. Additionally, I also have great memories as a young person growing up in the church arena, which was a great part of my family life.

Unexpectedly, my bubble got burst after my O-levels results, when I learnt to face life head-on. Sadly I missed the admission marks to join a national university by a few points. Therefore, I had to look for alternative studies. Hence, I decided to get into the hotel industry which I perceived as a ticket to go abroad. Kenya being a tourist destination, I assumed I would navigate my hospitality career out of the country as I had seen other successful hoteliers do. Nonetheless, my decision was a further disappointment to a few close acquaintances, who felt that the hotel career choice was demeaning to our family legacy of reputable professions. However, I was adamant to follow my dreams of going back to UK where I was born to further my studies.

Generally, I recollect starting off my career by working as a waitress in a hotel in Kenya, which was a hard job and not as glamorous as I initially thought. Then with the support of my family, I went on to study food technology diploma in Mombasa Polytechnic University College. After my diploma, I looked for a job in the food industry in Kenya with no avail. Eventually, I got a job as a lounge hostess at Jomo Kenyatta International airport. I have recollections of working night shifts, thereafter going for driving lessons in the morning after work, then going home to sleep for 5 hours and later going for French lessons before going back to work for an evening shift. It looked ridiculous to many because I could hardly afford a lot and now I was doing driving.... 'does she think she is going to be driving to work soon', some people wondered. But I had a dream!

My dreams were to get education to a doctorate level, go abroad to UK, succeed in a career, be married, become a mother, influence others positively, invest, live a Godly life and eventually go to Heaven. More than a decade after my goal planning, I can freely say that half of my dreams have come true. I have studied Psychology to master's degree in the UK and I am happily married living comfortably in London. I started my own business and I have influenced people positively through my EV-Online counselling services, among other accomplishments, and I am still working hard towards my dreams.

I don't share these dreams to show off, but I share them to encourage you that dreams come true. If you remain focussed, work hard and have faith, you will get there eventually. Sometimes, other people won't believe in your dreams, others will think you are deluded to even dream. Others might define you according to your colour, family background, talent, achievements or even your disabilities. Other times you might not have the resources or the knowhow to get them. But as Obama said in his book Audacity of Hope; 'I refuse to be defined by circumstances, failures, setbacks or others' opinion'. So never give up but keep going, you will find a way to the top.

Having alleged that I have got halfway my dreams doesn't mean it came easy, or it is easier now. For example, in my first month to coming to UK having achieved one of my goals which made my family so proud of me, my father died suddenly in Kenya. I got so confused whether to go back to Kenya and be with my family, or whether to stay and follow my dreams. However it was only wise to stay. Hence as I dealt with bereavement I decided to do what would have made my dad proud and have an education. Indeed, during five years of living in UK I had to work full-time and study part-time. Moreover, I had to take undergraduate study workload equivalent to full time study. I didn't sleep much, I didn't socialise much nor I didn't travel as much as I could have been if I wasn't doing this. Nevertheless, I don't count it loss, since I am at the climax of my academic voyage given that after this year' summer holidays, I will commence PhD studies at The Middlesex University. So, I am quite satisfied with my journey process.

However, it is not easy to get to your dreams, it requires a fighters' spirit. Sometimes you will fail but you have to wake up, dust off and keep going. I remember one time during my undergraduate I had to postpone one module because I couldn't afford it. Another time I was studying two modules consecutively, working full-time in mental health rehab and planning my wedding. As a result, I failed one paper which I couldn't re-sit, hence I had to re-do the whole module again. It took me some time to get back my balance, but guess what?... I did it.

Even so, having purported that I have achieved most of my dreams, I must admit that there are many people who supported me along the way. First is my family including; my parents and my brothers, my uncles and aunties, my cousins and also many friends who were excellent. Most of them stuck in the journey. Some friends were there in different seasons. I remember when I was doing my undergraduate and I had a few friends who were research students who were so gracious, supportive and helpful, may God bless them. I also recall my work managers and colleagues who allowed me to select my shifts and annual leaves to suit my study programmes. I recall friends who organised my graduation parties, my wedding and those who sat with me when I planned my dreams, proof read my work and also gave constructive feedback. I really appreciate them all.

Overall, my message to you today is to encourage you to follow your dreams. Nothing is impossible, but nothing worth having comes easy. Position yourself in the right places and with the right people. If the going gets tough, rest, reflect and wake up then continue. Ask for help when you need it. Make your dreams and visions into goals, and then make SMART steps that will help you reach your goals. All things are possible to those who believe and go after them.

Remember, **where there is a will there is a way**.

RULES THAT AIDED MY JOURNEY;

1 .**PASSION**- Knowing my passion for psychology, education and for helping others live productive healthy lives helped me define my goals. I listened to documentaries and programmes and further read books and research papers that rejuvenate my passion. Reviewing my goals also keeps my passion in check especially in tough times.

2. SUPPORT- Good backing from my family members, friends, workmates, mentors and role models kept me going. My family have been a great moral support and they also advised me when making major decisions. I also identified several mentors whom I learnt a lot from.

3. FAITH- My Christian faith helped me a lot. I prayed consistently for my goals and I asked others to pray for me. Faith gave me the strength to believe in my goals and to believe that God had given me a life of purpose. The Christianity doctrines laid the fundamental principles for my life, especially through reading the book of Proverbs, which is full of wisdom and guidance.

4. RESILIENCE- Even in tough times like during financial difficulties, or times of loneliness and bereavement seasons or even the times that I made mistakes, I still remained focused. I have always tried my best to be strong and to maintain upright character. Following the rules and the laws was essential.

5.MOTIVATION- I learnt from a young age that in order to achieve, I had to keep on encouraging myself. Sometimes no-one believed in my goals, other times people forgot them or made fun of them, but I kept pushing on till I conquered.

6.ASSOCIATION- Over the years, I have sought different associations with people of like mind. Sometimes I had to cut off some friendships in order for me to progress.

8.PLANNING- Life management and planning my goals has been essential. I have always done a time plan for my life, I write down how I hope to spend every week's hours at the start of every year and I review my plan regularly as outlined on time management topic in this book ie 8 hours of reading, 6 hours with family , 6 hours resting etc. I also plan my long term and short term goals and monitor progress closely.

9. PERSONAL ANALYSIS- one advantage of studying psychology was learning to psychoanalyse myself. My studies helped me to be self-aware of my strengths and weaknesses. I have also been able to deal with difficult emotions of hurt, grief and disappointment over the years. Liberating myself from negative lifestyles as a result I ushered in progress, happiness and health.

I wish you good luck with your dreams and goals into achieving a fulfilled living. I hope in your journey to success you can meditate on this quote by Ben Carson: *"Success is not determined by whether or not you face obstacles, but by your reaction. If you look at obstacles as containing fences then, they become your excuse for failure.* **But** *if you look at them as hurdles, each one of them will strengthen you for the next level."*

CONCLUDING REMARKS:

STEPPING INTO THE FUTURE

As we come to the end of the book, it is important to evaluate the skills you have learnt and identify areas that need more input. Then, do your best to put into practice what you have learnt. Look into the future with a smile of hope that it will get better. The past is gone but what you do to today determine the route you take.

EVALUATION CHECKLIST

(Where are you in these areas of life?)

MAINTAINING THE WHOLE

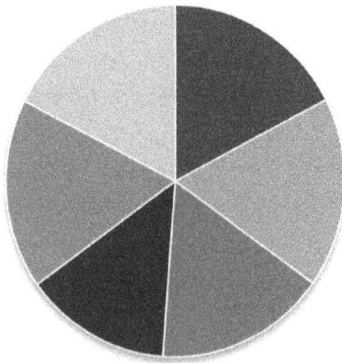

- Physical health
- Psychological health
- Relationships
- Dreams& Goals
- Hope, Faith,happiness
- Stress Mngt

SCORES- 1. Very Good   2. Good   3. Average   4.Poor 5. Very poor

It is advisable to revisit the wellbeing checklist in the introduction chapter to evaluate where you are now and also to help you identify areas you need to put in extra effort. The categories that you have scored **3, 4 and 5** needs more input and you can read again the chapters that outline them.

Progress Planner
(Where do you need MORE Effort?)

	STRENGTHS	WEAKNESSES	ACTION PLAN	REVIEW DATE
Physical Health				
Psychological Health				
Relationships				
Dreams/Goals/Success				
Stress Management				
Hope/Faith/Happiness				
Other				

1. Use the table above to **prepare an action plan** on different AREAS that need more effort.

2. Put the plan in a **place** you can see it regularly.

3. **Practice daily**, the skills you have learnt to attain the goal plan.

4. **Review** your plan after a few months, to monitor progress.

Finally, I would like to remind you that **Success, Health and Happiness are not attained in a day, but it is work in progress.** Whatever you honour and observe on a regular basis will shape your life outcomes. It is possible to free ourselves from destructive patterns and achieve positive habits for superior outcomes, if we are persistent.

Therefore:-

- Aim to enjoy your everyday life, appreciating the people in your life and the achievements you have gained so far.
- Aim to learn something useful every day.
- Look after yourself through healthy eating, exercise, positive thinking and good association.
- Never suppress issues, deal with them promptly and effectively.
- Nurture your hope, faith, talents and opportunities.
- Regularly take time to have fun, to rest and also to reflect and to plan for future goals.

Ambition to live a fulfilled life where you are healthier, successful and happy.

STUDIES & STATISTICS REFERENCES

Alcohol Concern UK (2011); *www.alcoholconcern.org.uk*

Bandura, A. (1977). Social Learning Theory. *Englewood Cliffs, NJ: Prentice Hall.*

Carlson N 2007 ; Physiology of behaviour; *Pearson international*

Guardian newspaper UK 2011; *www-the-guardian-uk.com*

Kramer and Ellen 2003; A Survival Analysis of Timing of Entry into Prostitution: *Sociological inquiry vol 73,p 511-528*

MIND UK ; www.mind.org.uk

NHS (2011); *www.nhs.uk*

NCHA(2011); *www.acha-ncha.org*

Saffrey J , Stewart M 1997, Maintaining The whole, Human Biology and health; *Open University*

Vygotsky L (1978) Thought and language; *Cambridge MA, MIT press*

W.H.O 2000; World health organisation ranking of health systems; *http://www.photius.com/rankings/healthranks.html*